Rachel Kneebone: Regarding Rodin

Rachel Kneebone: Regarding Rodin

With text by Ali Smith
Foreword by Catherine Morris

Anomie Publishing

Foreword

The exhibition – an experiment in juxtaposition between two artists whose work intersects in remarkable ways – was suggested to Rachel Kneebone (b. 1973) by me. After accepting the invitation the process of conceiving and executing the show became a seamless collaborative effort. The idea was simple: present Kneebone's complex porcelain work alongside iconic bronzes by the nineteenth-century French master, François-Auguste-René Rodin (1840–1917), offering a formal dialogue, not outside of time or history, but across them. The creative exchange between these two sculptors was inspired by the unique convergence within the Brooklyn Museum of both an exceptional Rodin collection, gifted to the Museum in 1984 by the Iris and B. Gerald Cantor Foundation, and the Elizabeth A. Sackler Center for Feminist Art, which is committed to fostering expanded readings of works of art beyond traditional collection and historical boundaries, encouraging a theoretical engagement with looking, and looking differently. The pairing is intended to highlight interests shared by these two artists – born more than one hundred and thirty years apart – in using figurative sculpture to explore and represent the inextricable human experiences of sexuality, desire, loss and despair.

Catherine Morris
Sackler Family Curator
Elizabeth A. Sackler Center for Feminist Art, Brooklyn Museum

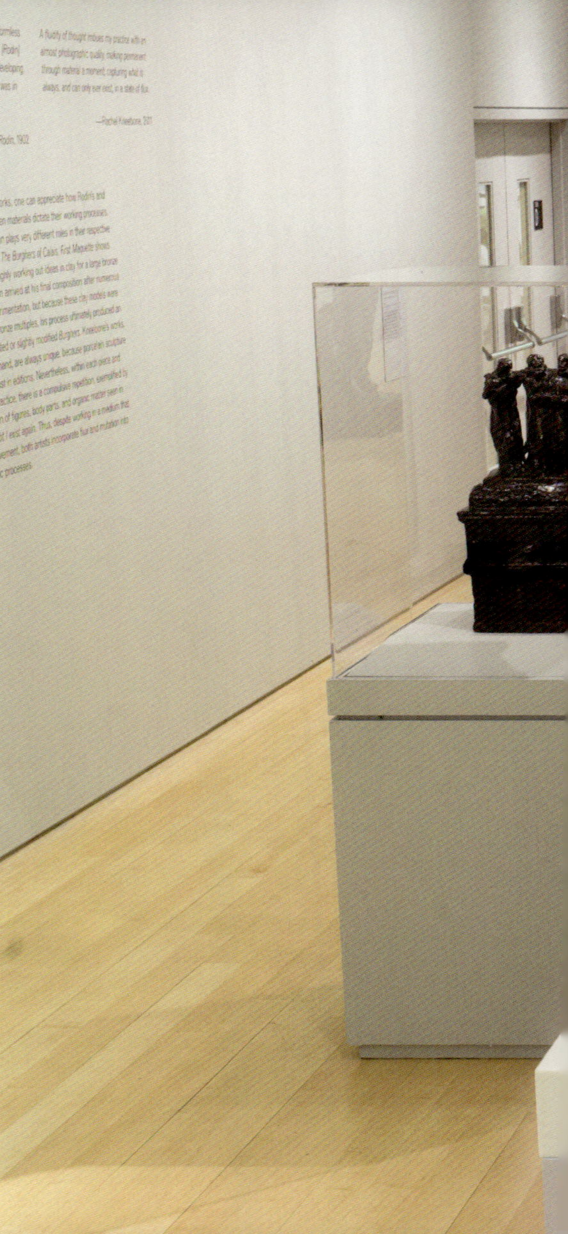
A fluidity of thought imbues my practice with an almost photographic quality, making permanent through material a moment, capturing what is always, and can only ever exist, in a state of flux.

—Rachel Kneebone, 2011

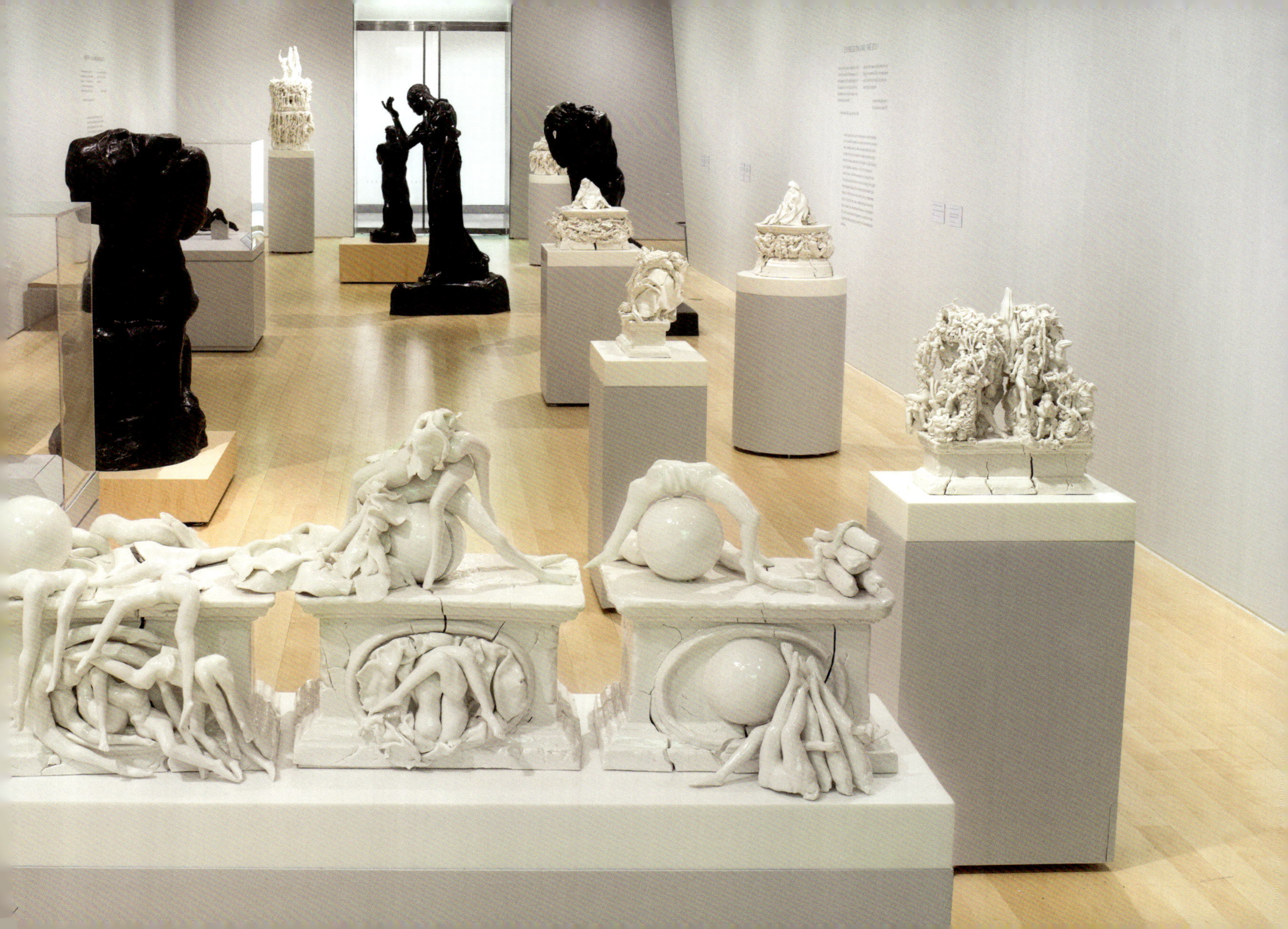

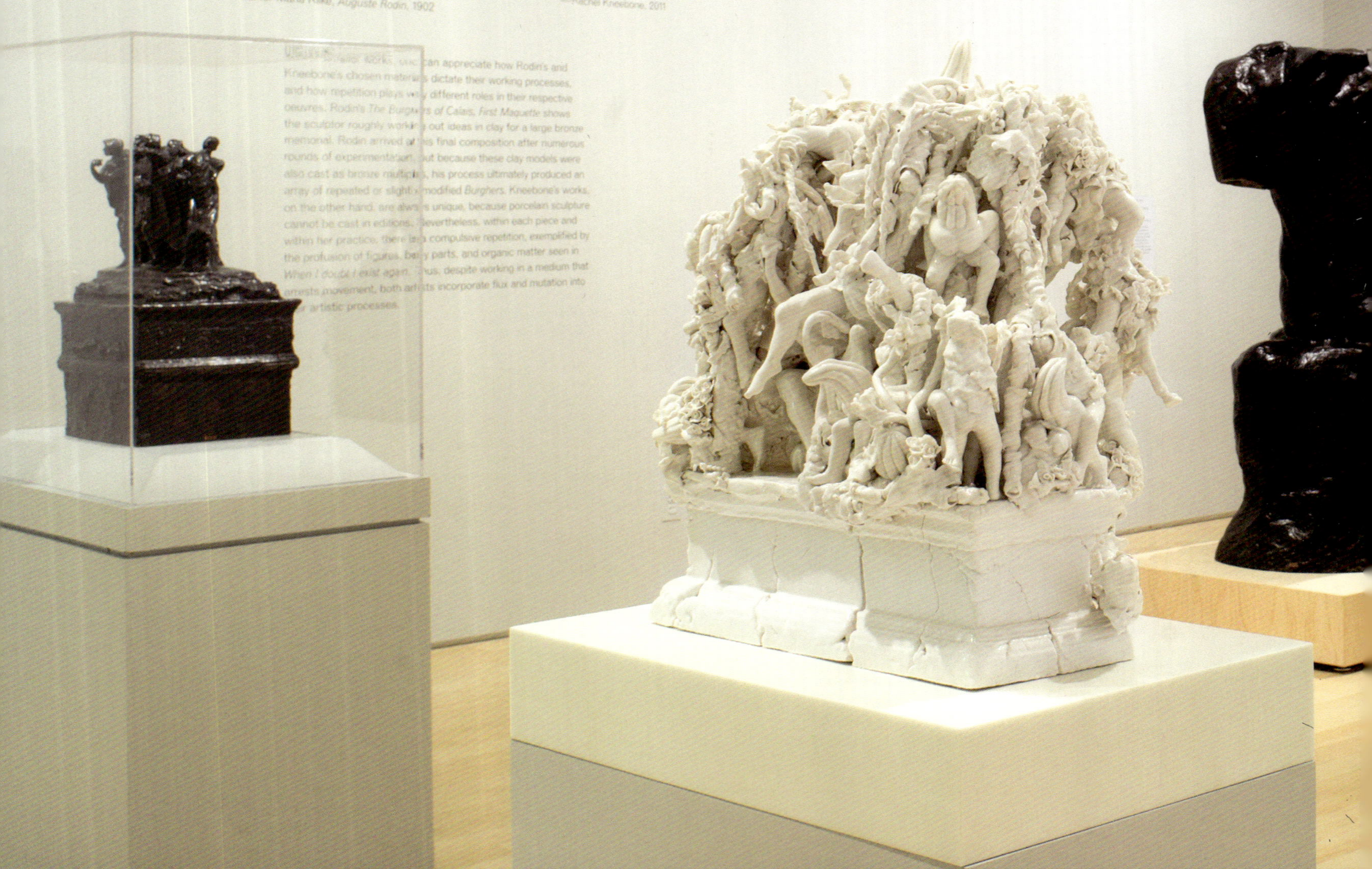
The inner life that makes up this age is formless
and intangible; it is, in short, in flux. . . . [Rodin]
took hold of everything that was vague, developing,
and constantly changing—all of which was in
him too—and gave form to it.
—Rainer Maria Rilke, Auguste Rodin, 1902
A fluidity of thought imbues my practice with an
almost photographic quality, making permanent
through material a moment; capturing what is
always, and can only ever exist, in a state of flux.
—Rachel Kneebone, 2011
Using these works, one can appreciate how Rodin's and Kneebone's chosen materials dictate their working processes, and how repetition plays very different roles in their respective oeuvres. Rodin's The Burghers of Calais, First Maquette shows the sculptor roughly working out ideas in clay for a large bronze memorial. Rodin arrived at his final composition after numerous rounds of experimentation, but because these clay models were also cast as bronze multiples, his process ultimately produced an array of repeated or slightly modified Burghers. Kneebone's works, on the other hand, are always unique, because porcelain sculpture cannot be cast in editions. Nevertheless, within each piece and within her practice, there is a compulsive repetition, exemplified by the profusion of figures, body parts, and organic matter seen in When I doubt I exist again. Thus, despite working in a medium that arrests movement, both artists incorporate flux and mutation into their artistic processes.

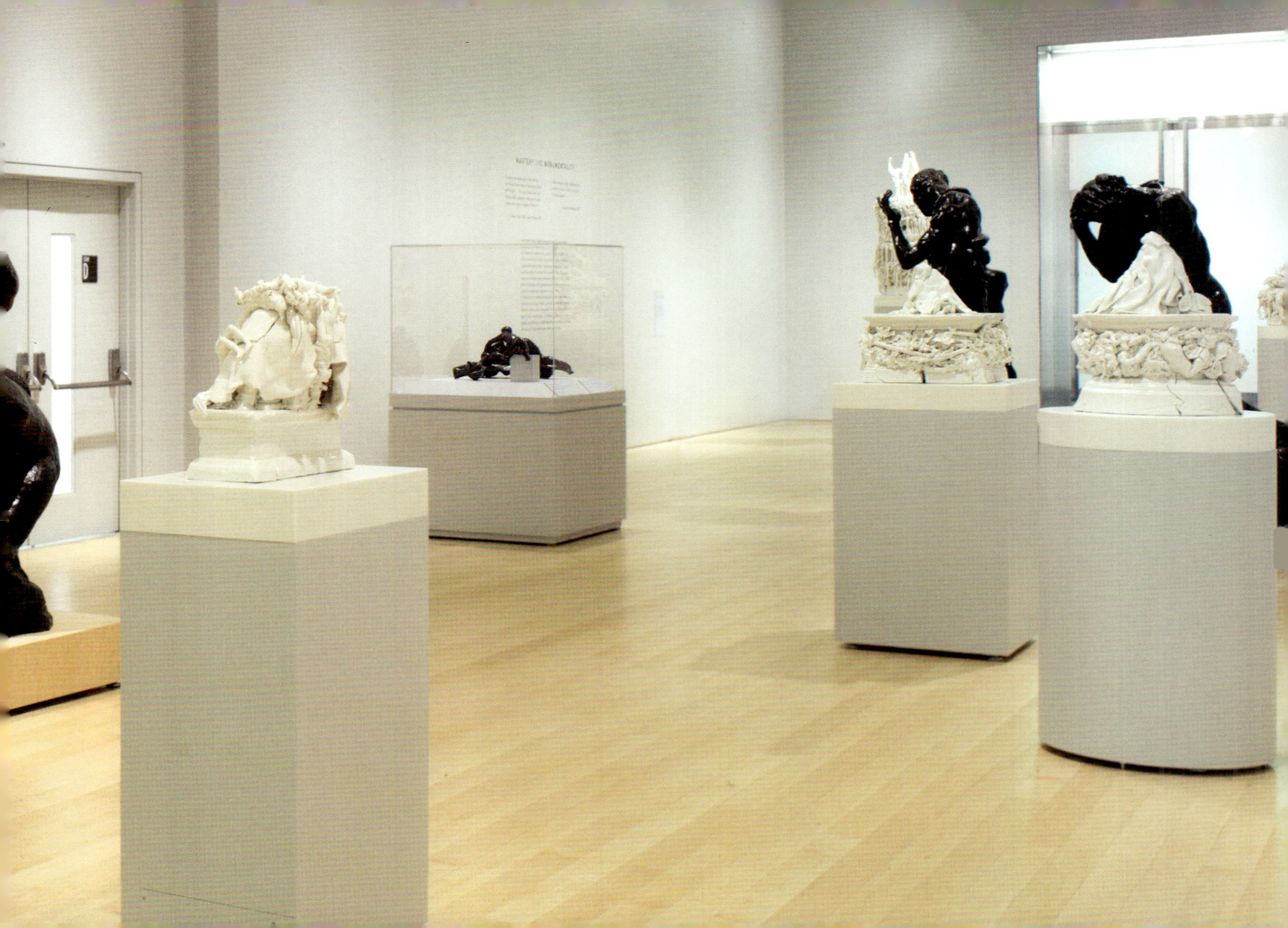

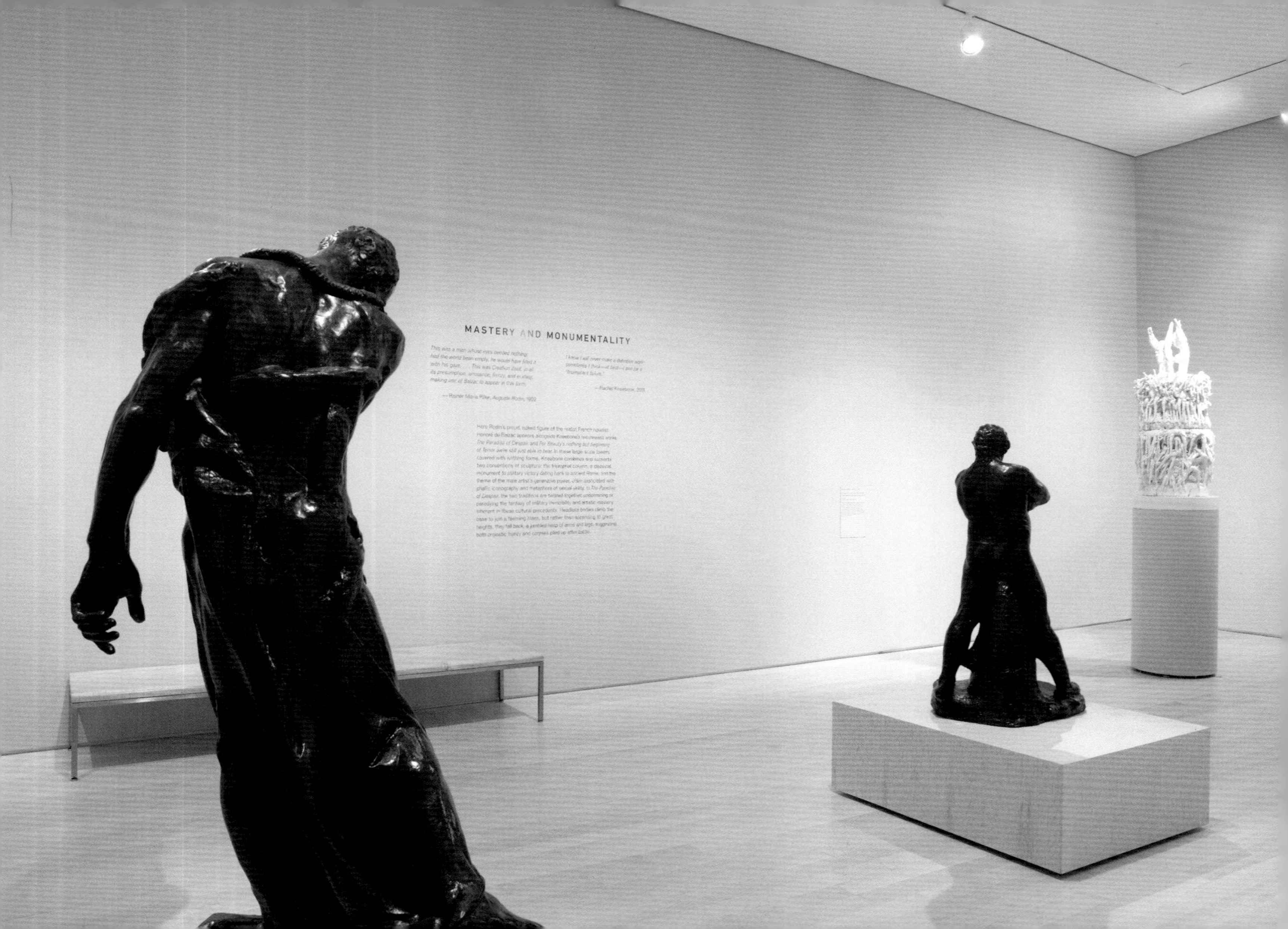

MASTERY AND MONUMENTALITY
This was a man whose eyes needed nothing; had the world been empty, he would have filled it with his gaze. ... This was Creation itself, in all its presumption, arrogance, frenzy, and ecstasy, making use of Balzac to appear in this form.
—Rainer Maria Rilke, Auguste Rodin, 1902
I know I will never make a definitive work—sometimes I think—at best—I aim for a "triumphant failure."
—Rachel Kneebone, 2011
Here Rodin's proud, naked figure of the realist French novelist Honoré de Balzac appears alongside Kneebone's two newest works, The Paradise of Despair and For Beauty's nothing but beginning of Terror we're still just able to bear. In these large-scale towers, covered with writhing forms, Kneebone combines and subverts two conventions of sculpture: the triumphal column, a classical monument to military victory dating back to ancient Rome, and the theme of the male artist's generative power, often associated with phallic iconography and metaphors of sexual virility. In The Paradise of Despair, the two traditions are twisted together, undermining or parodying the fantasy of military immortality and artistic mastery inherent in these cultural precedents. Headless bodies climb the base to join a teeming mass, but rather than ascending to great heights, they fall back, a jumbled heap of arms and legs, suggesting both orgiastic frenzy and corpses piled up after battle.

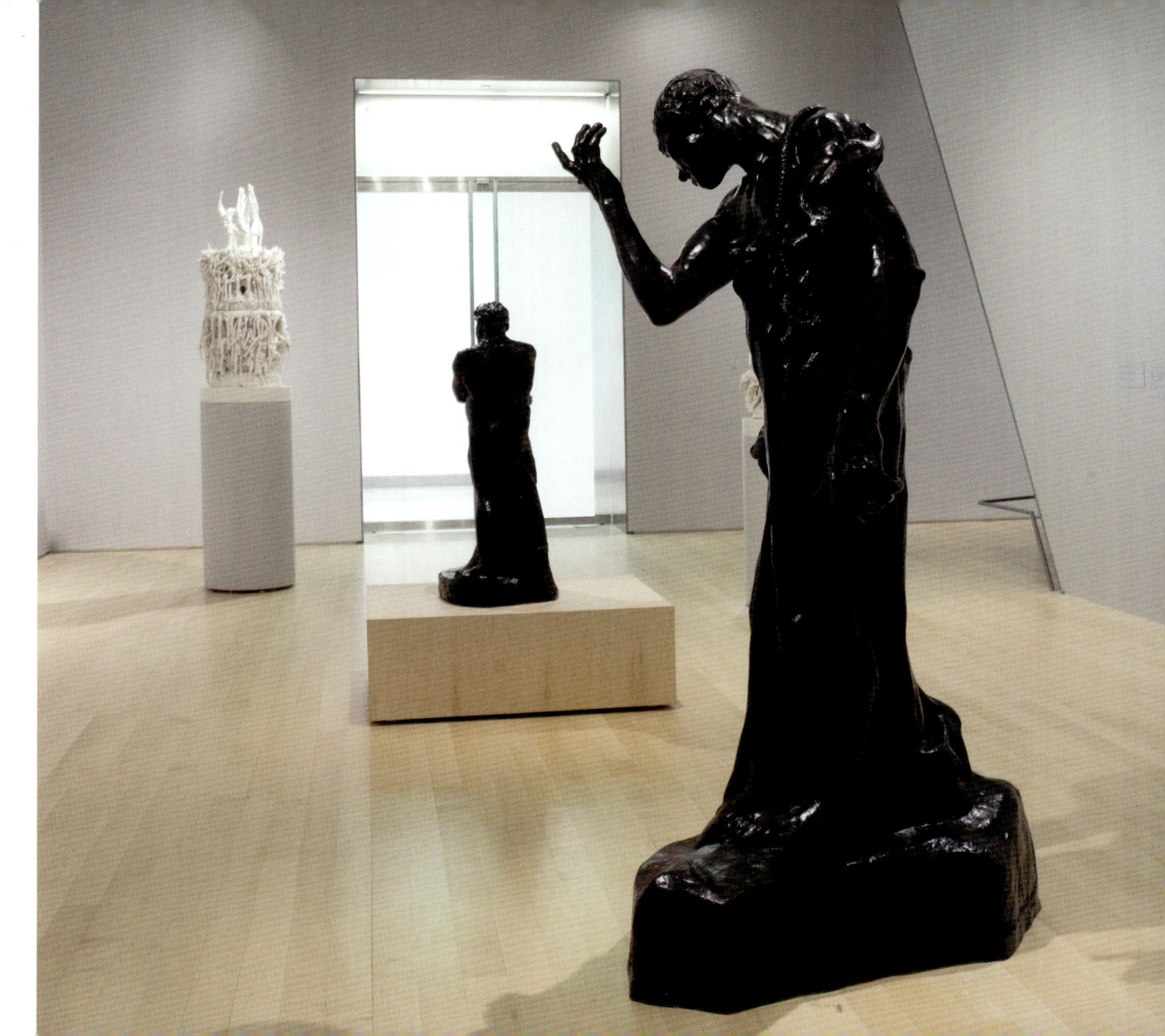

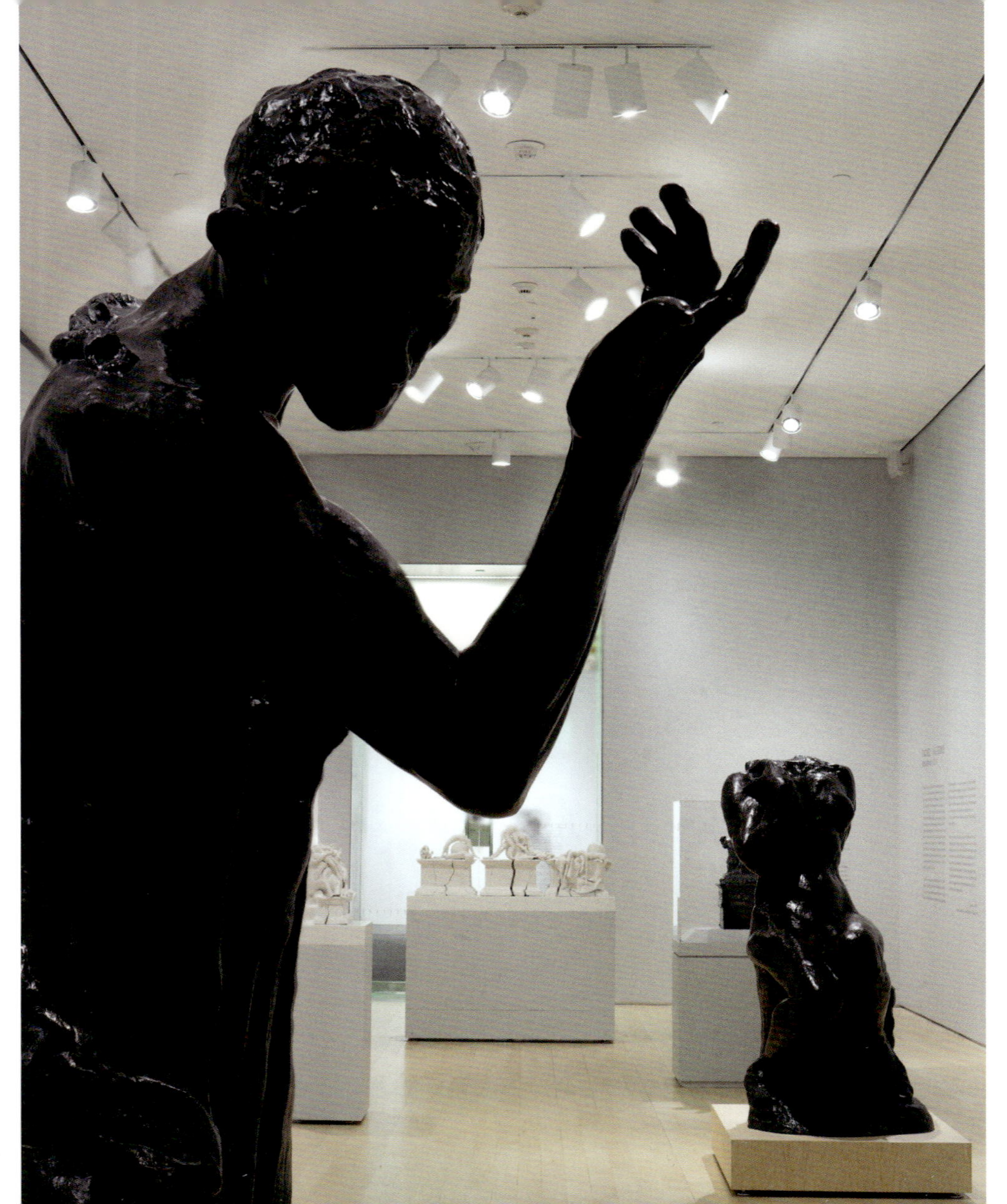

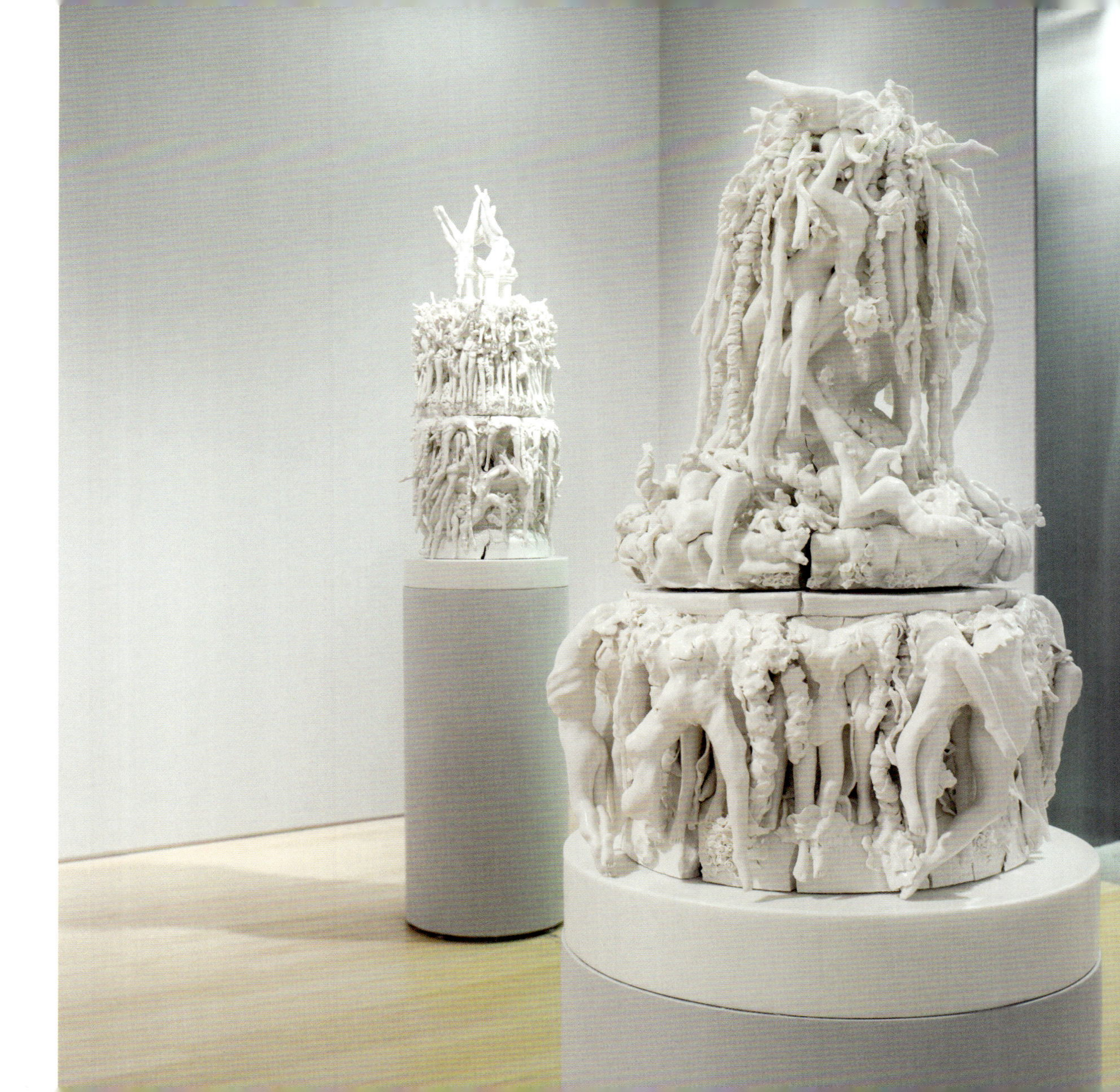

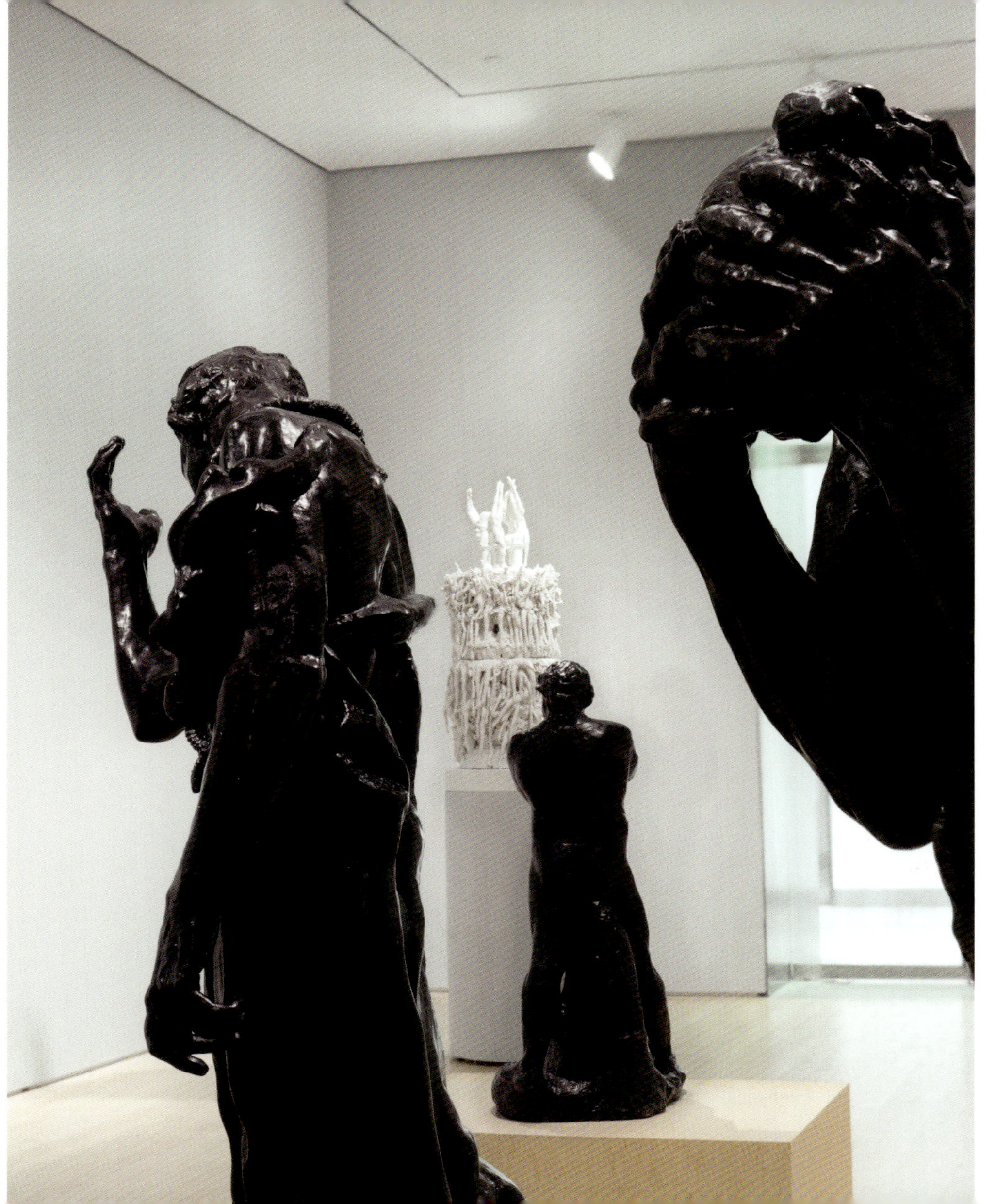

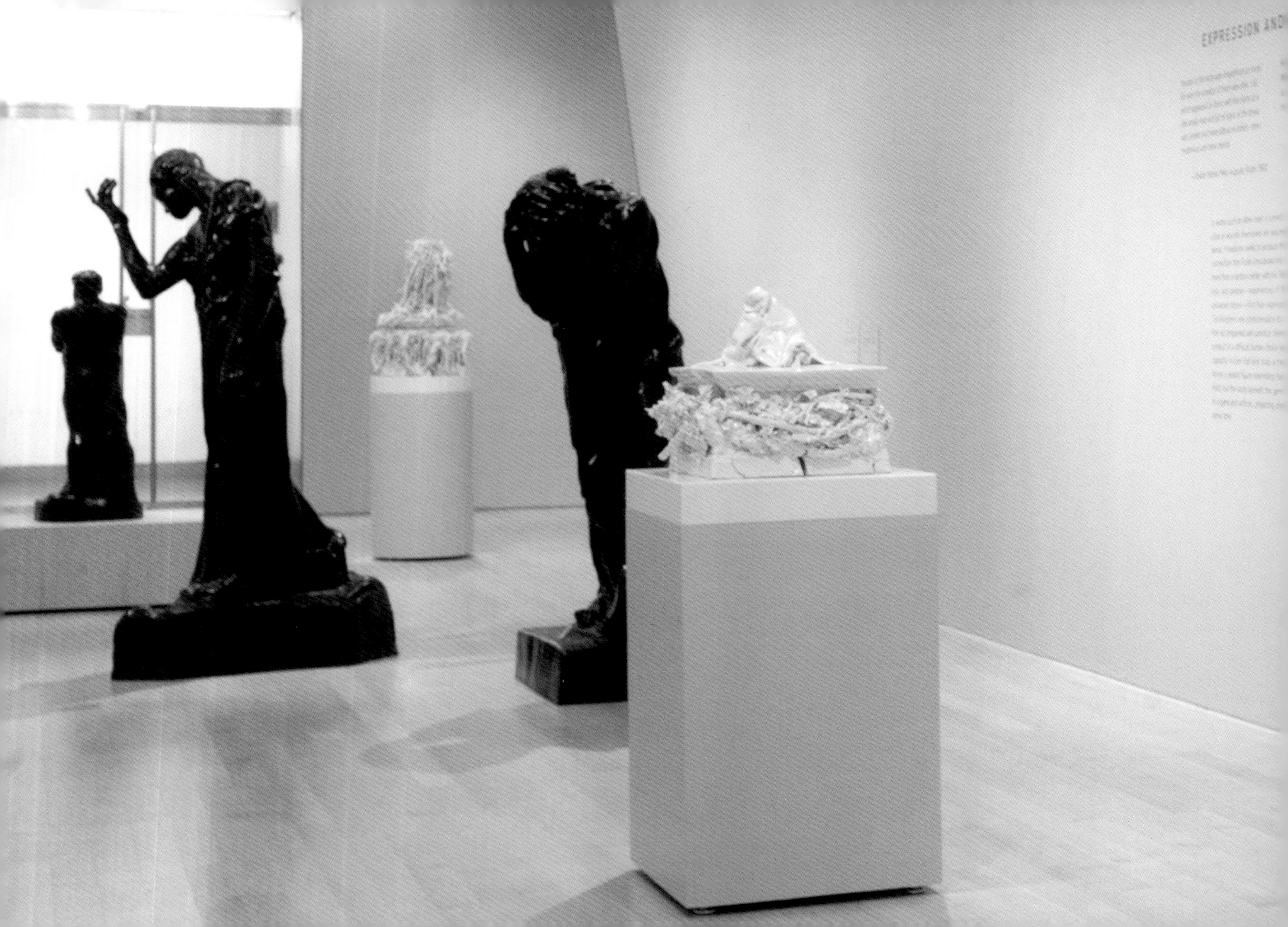

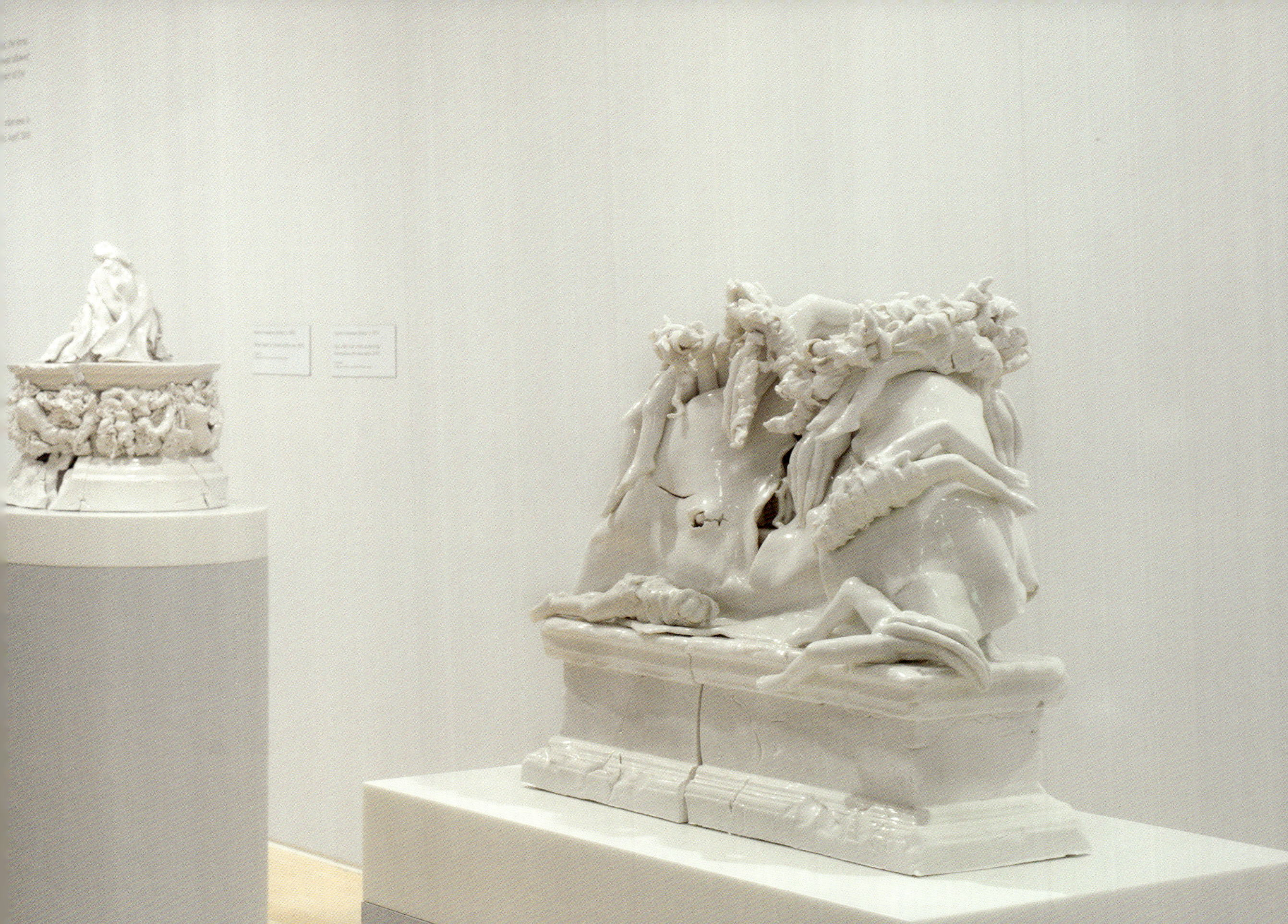

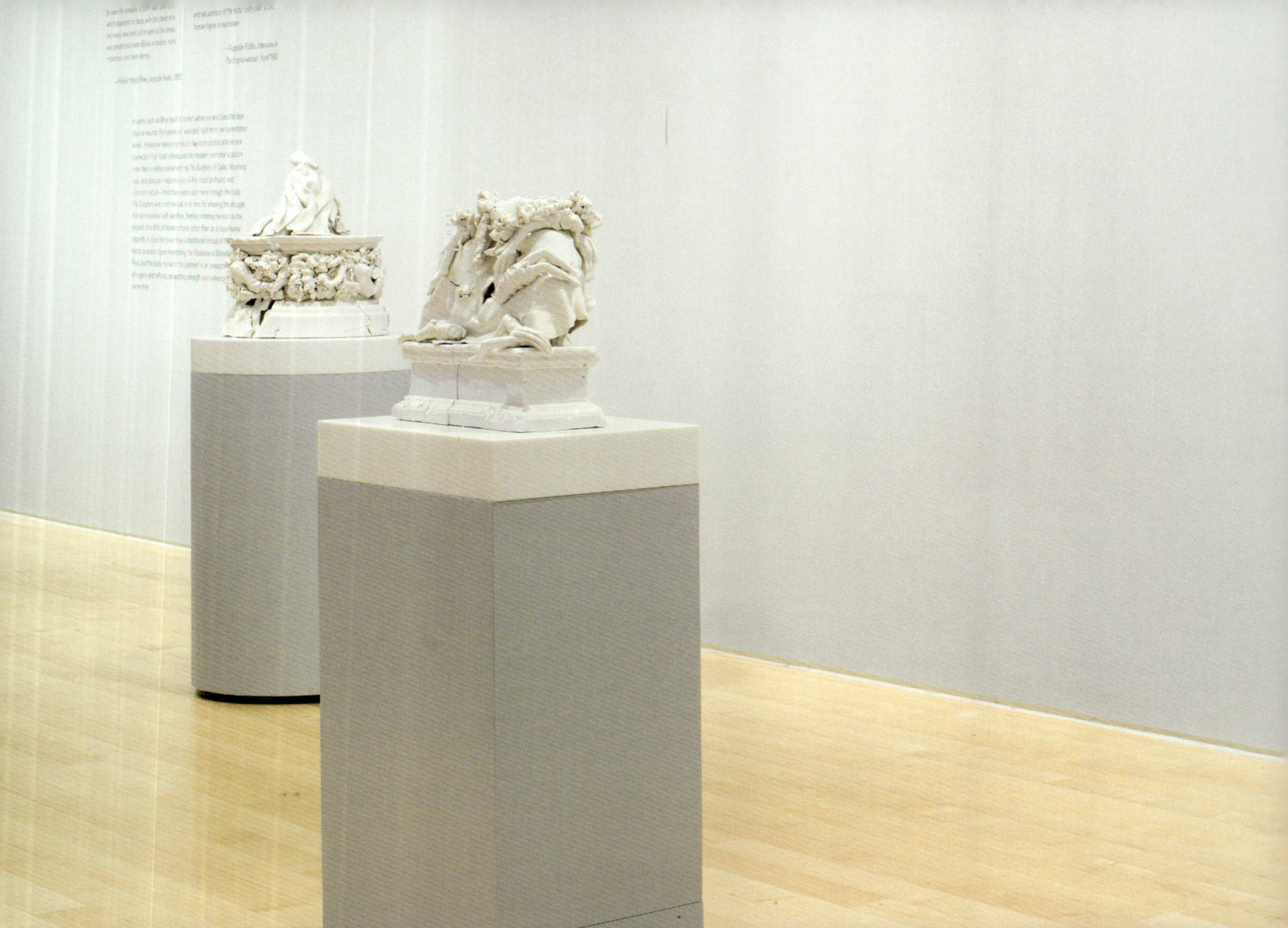

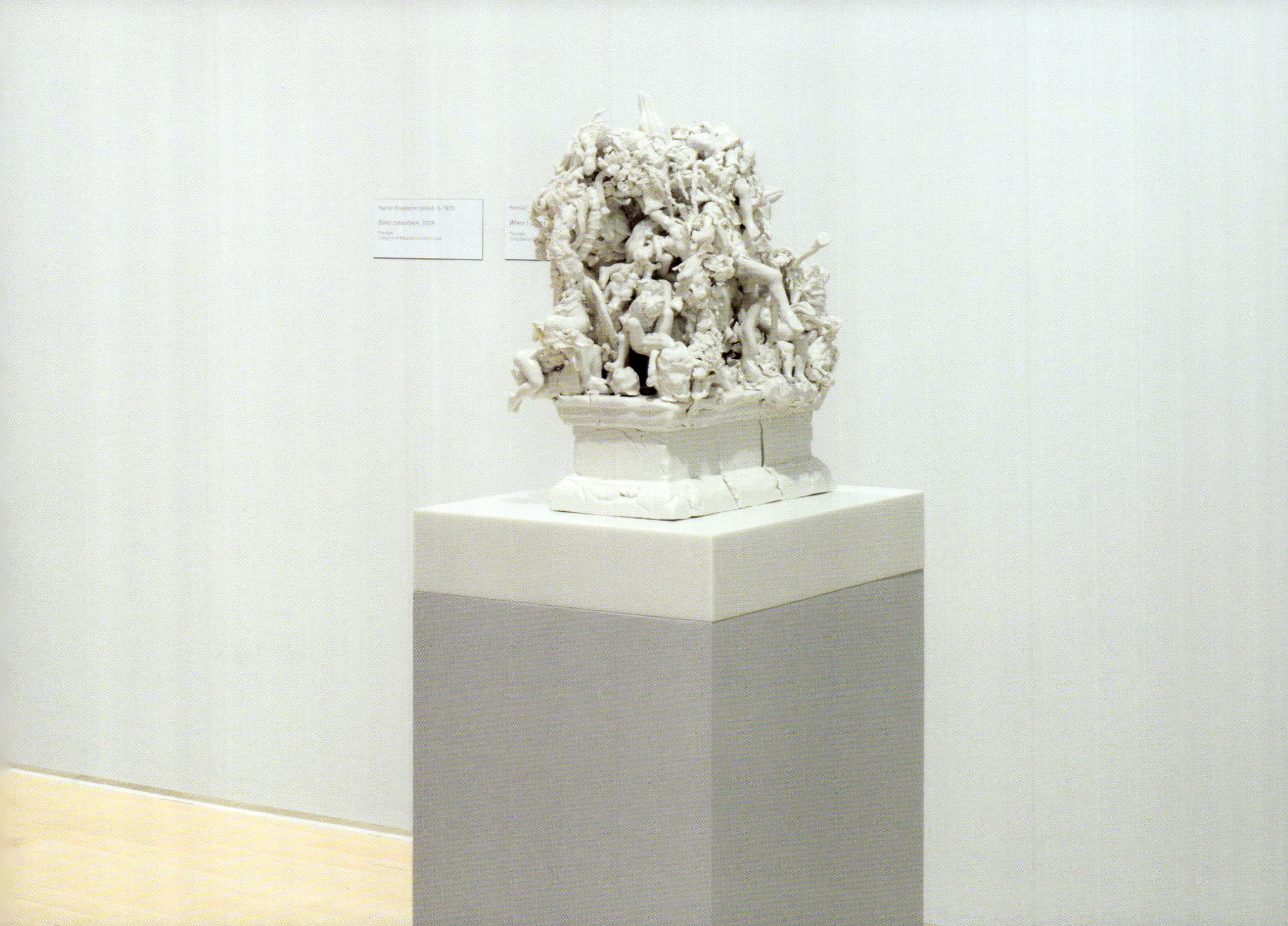

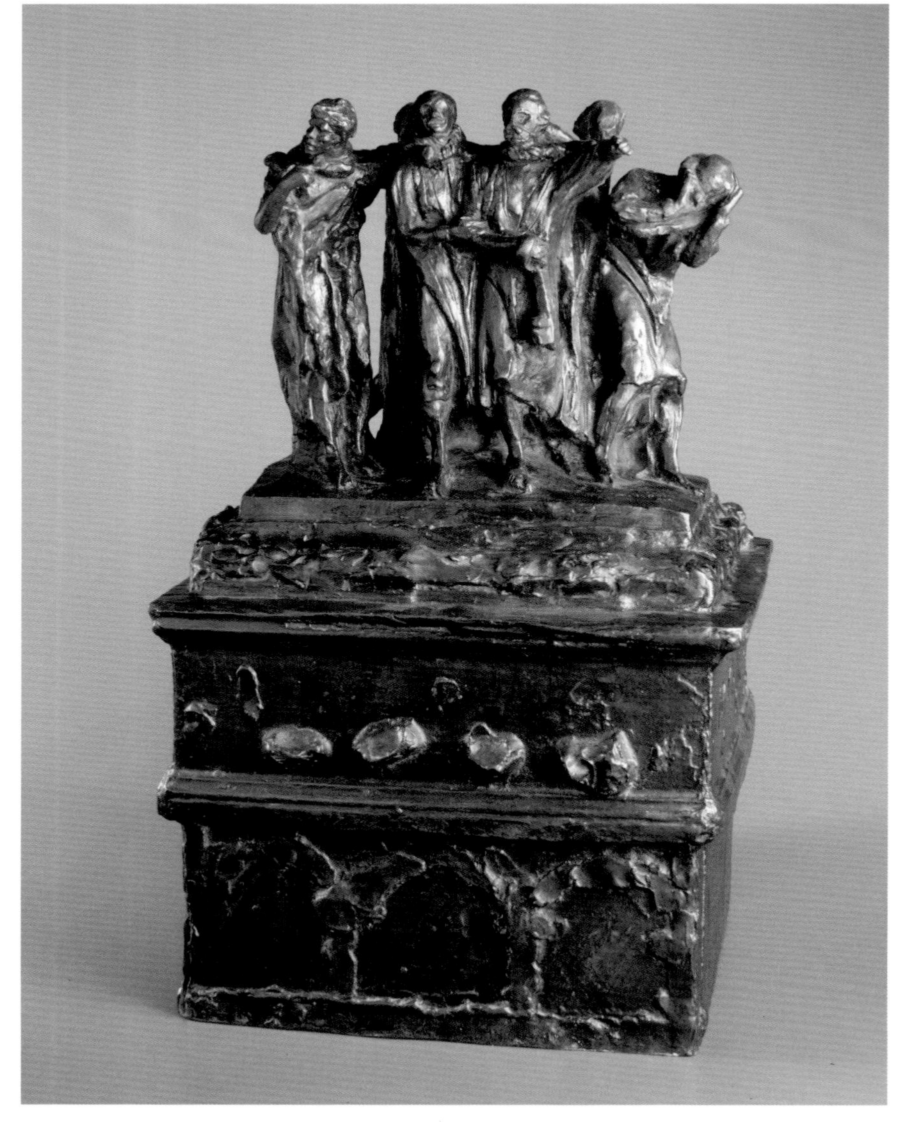

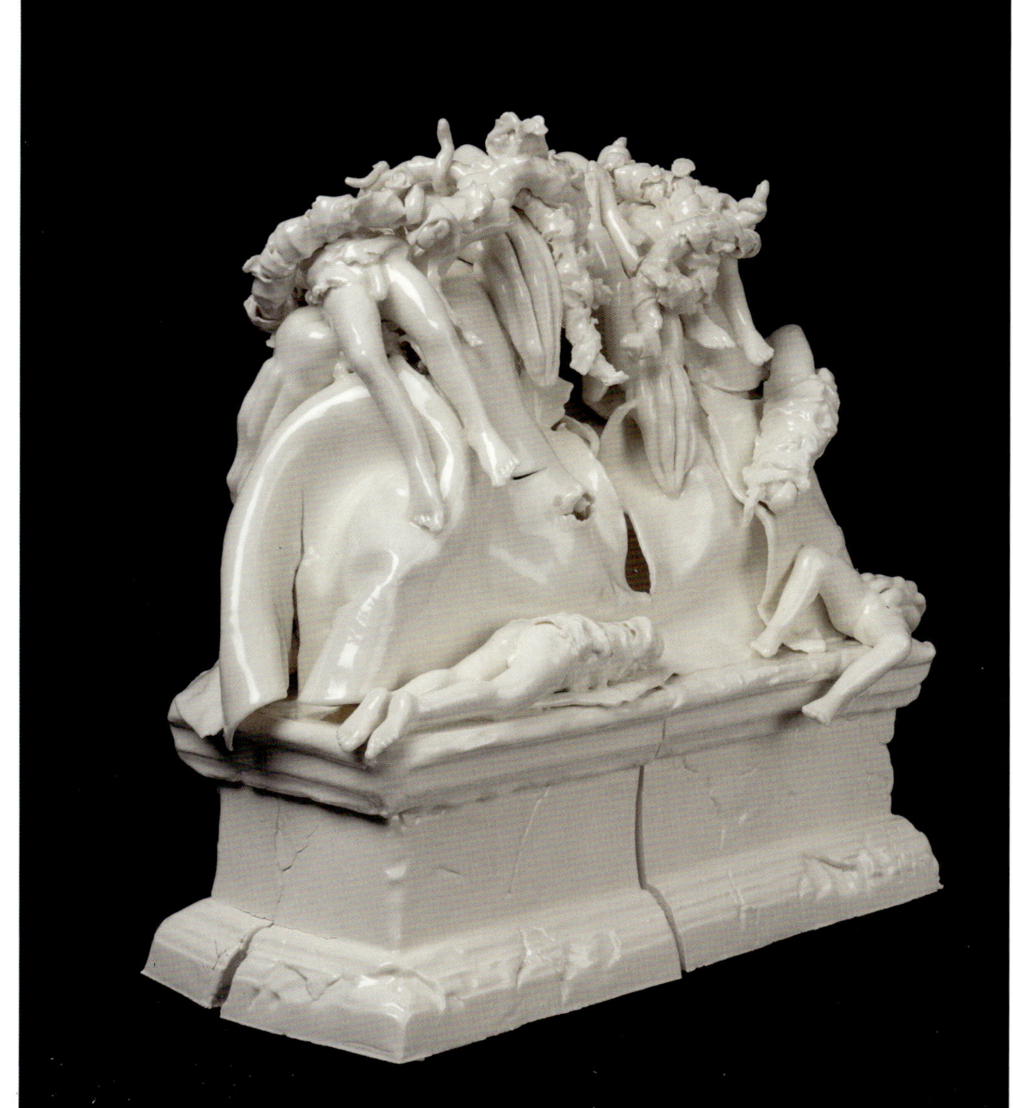

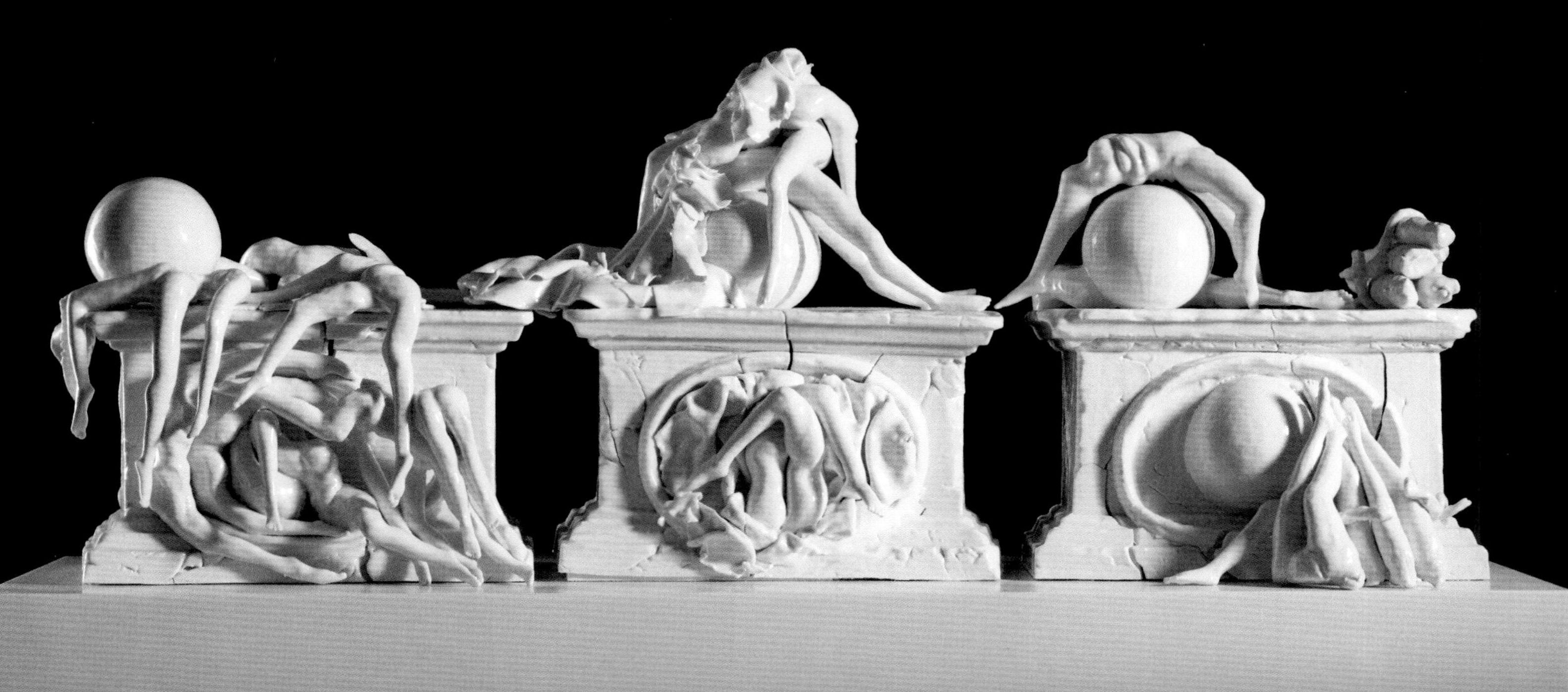

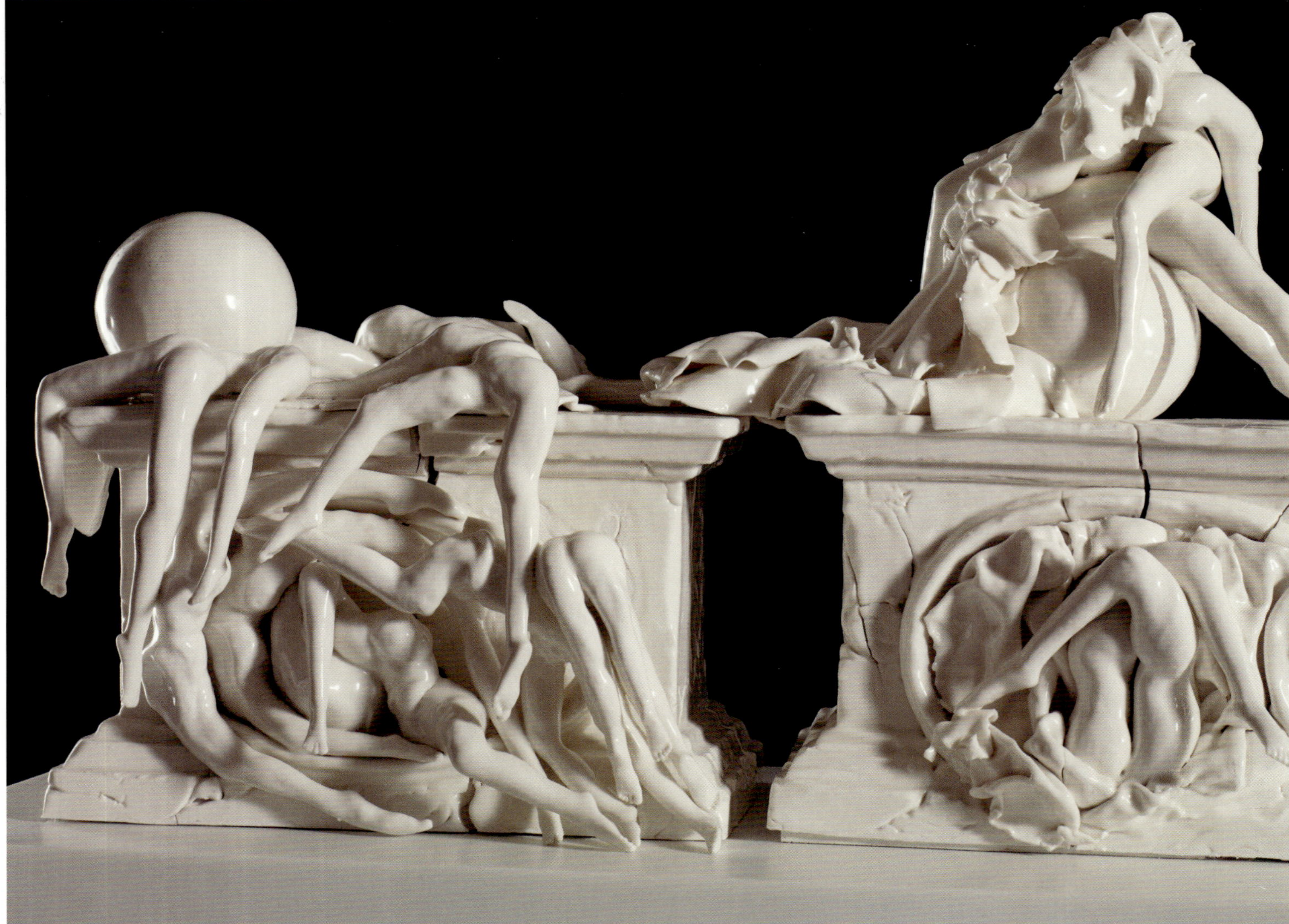

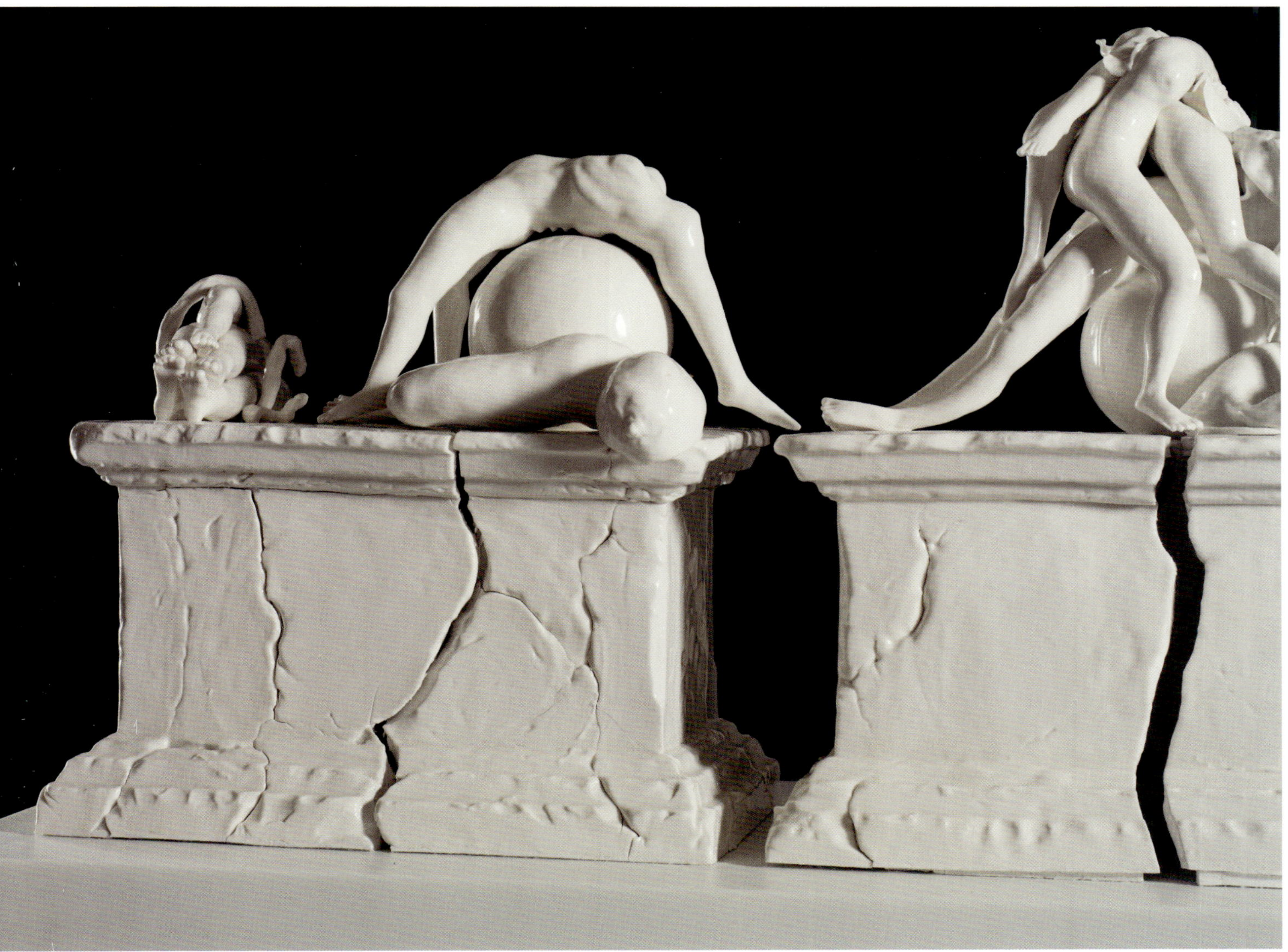

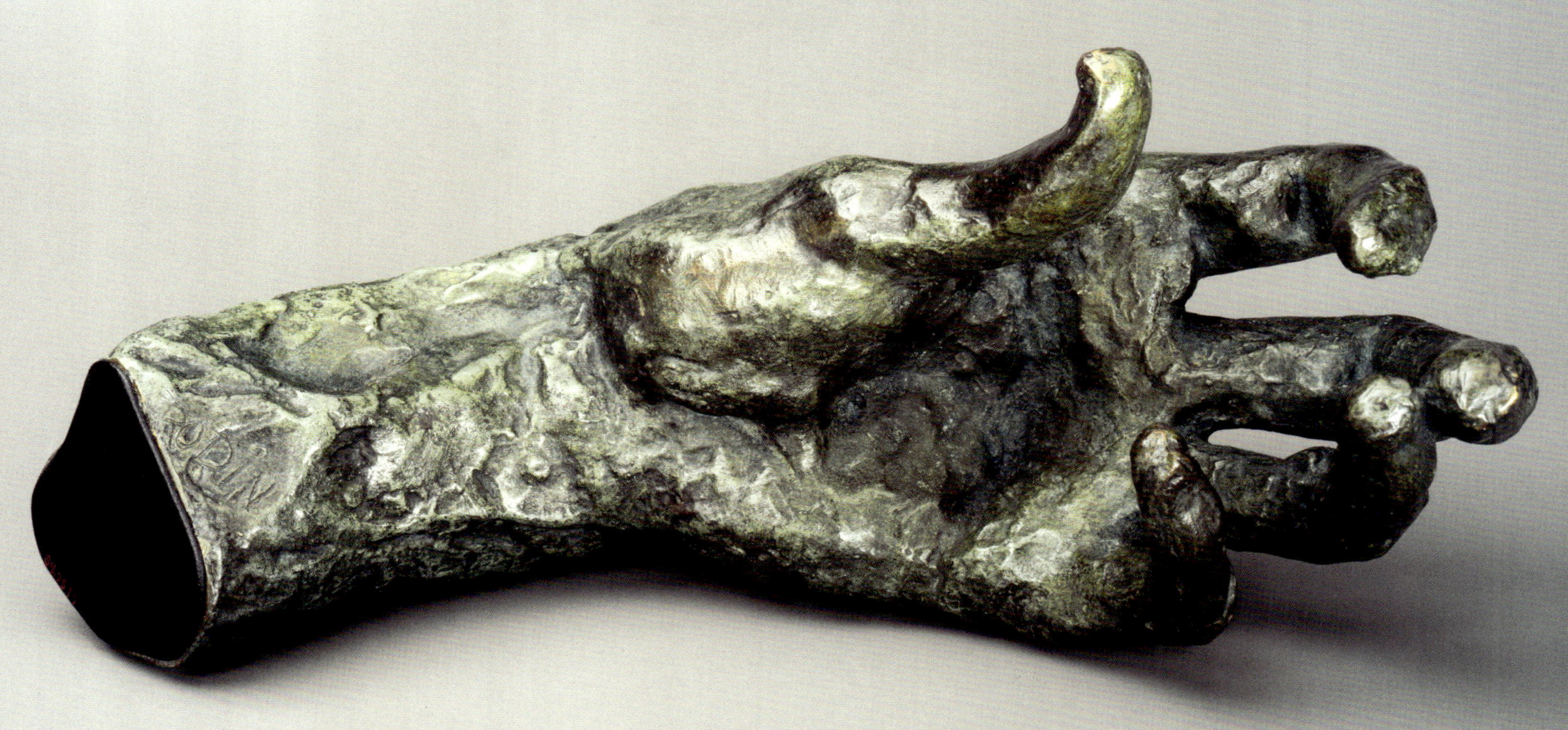

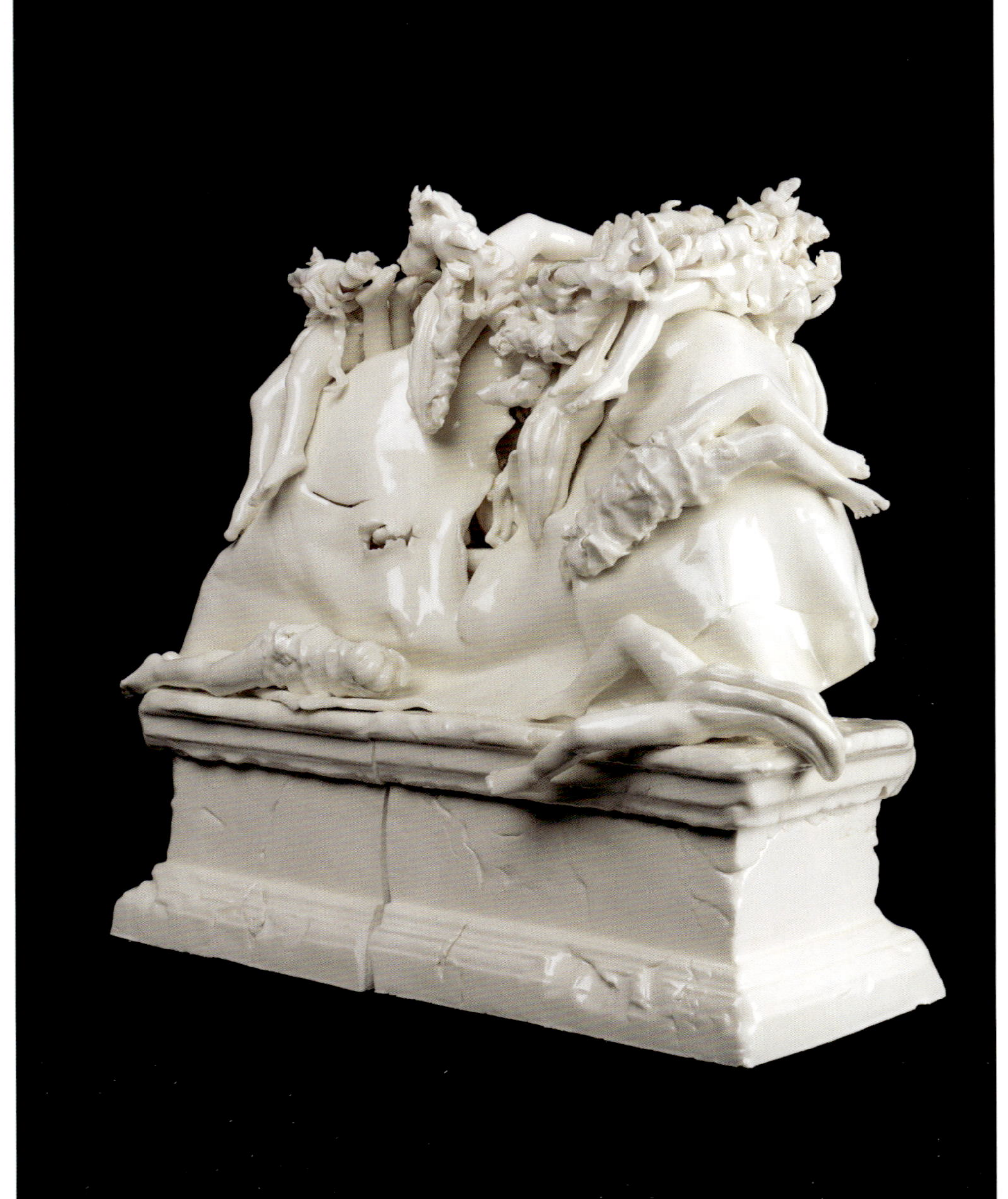

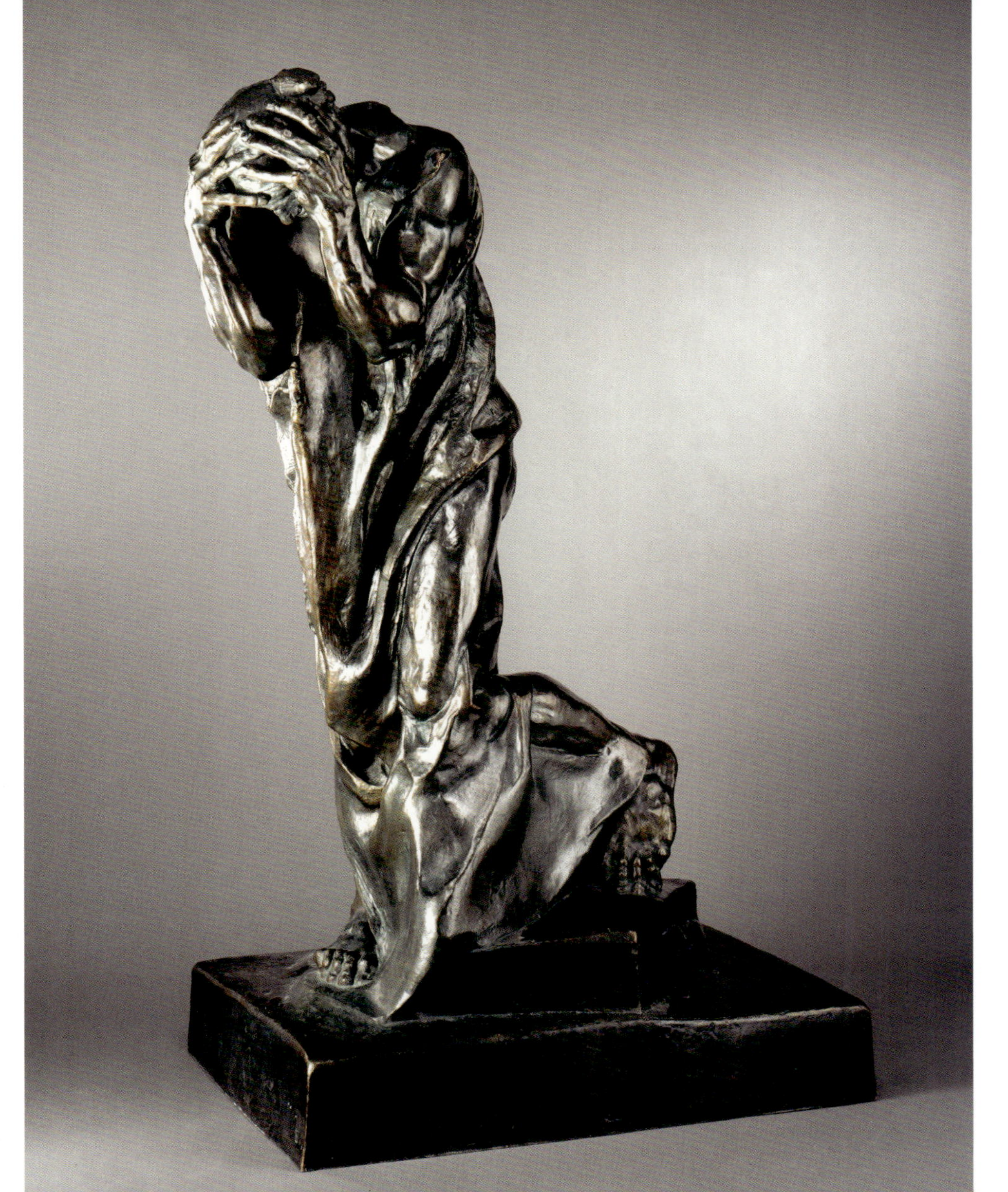

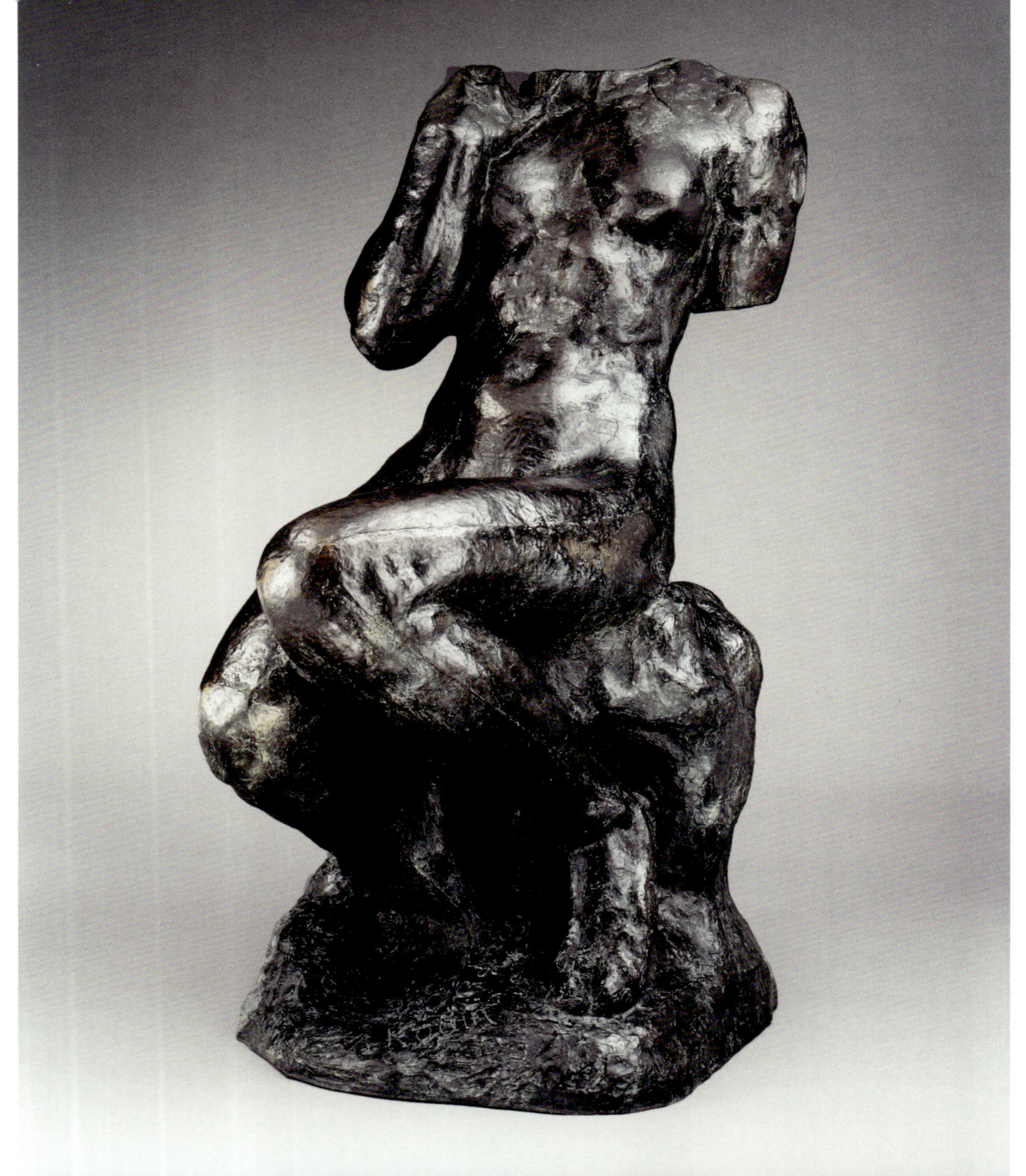

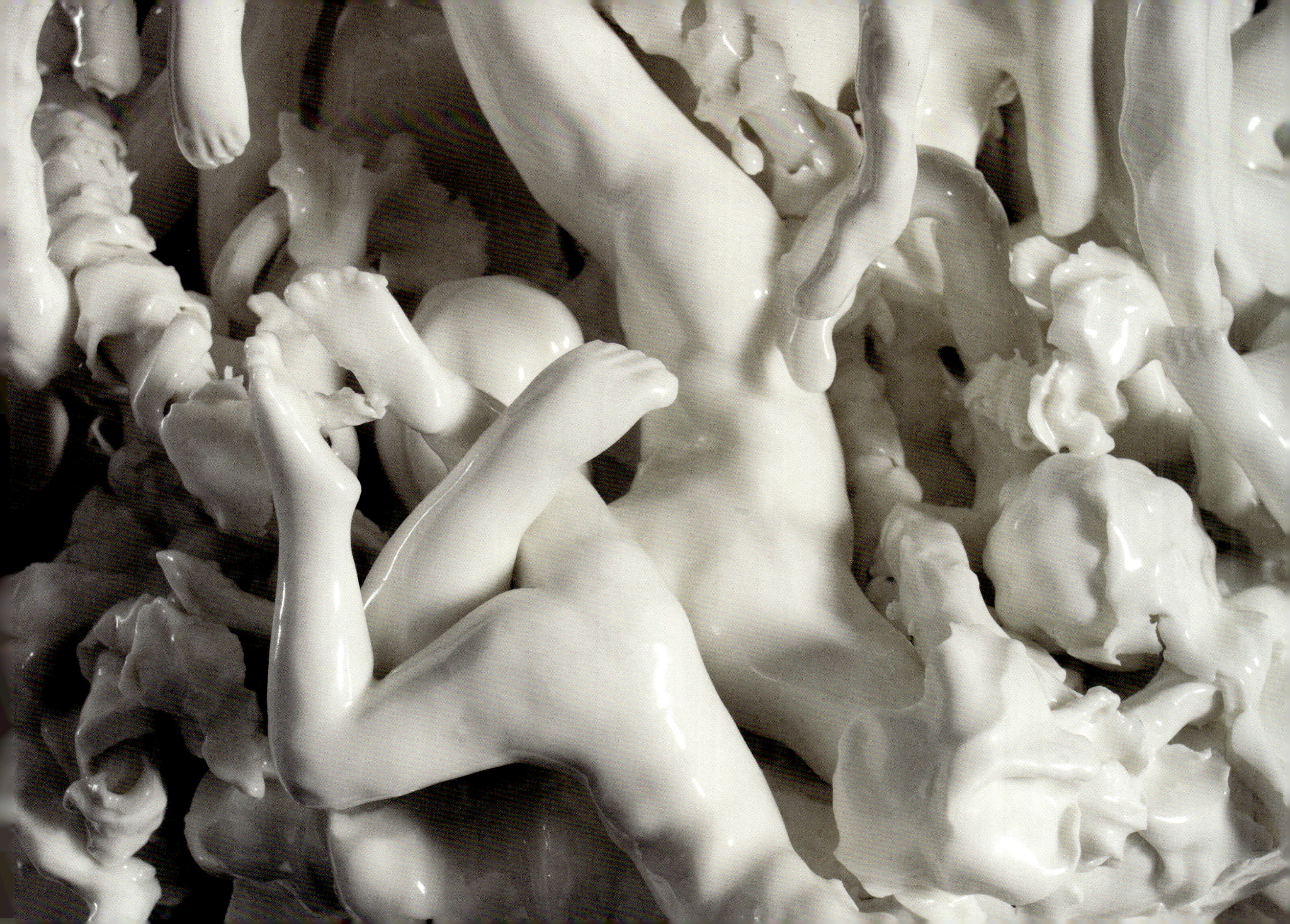

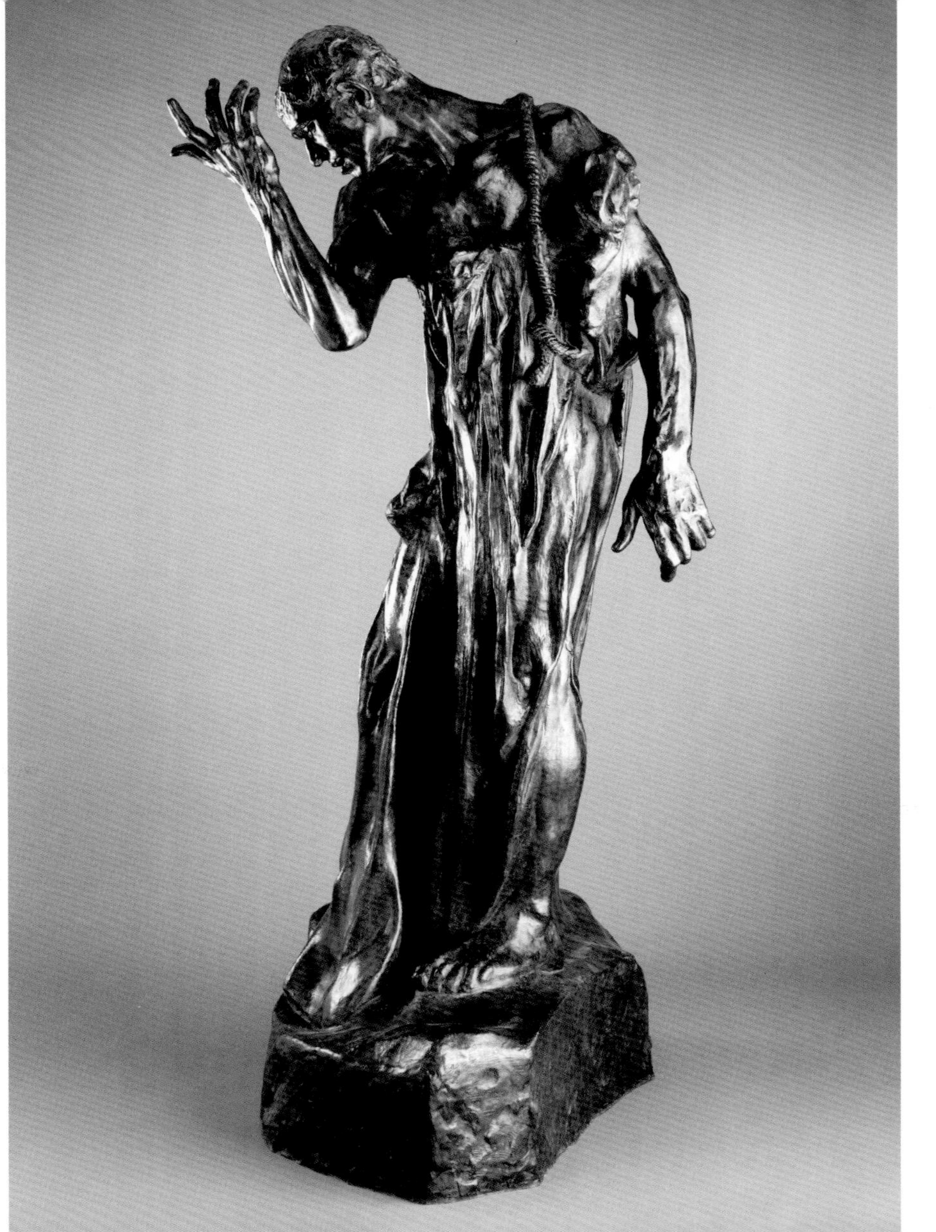

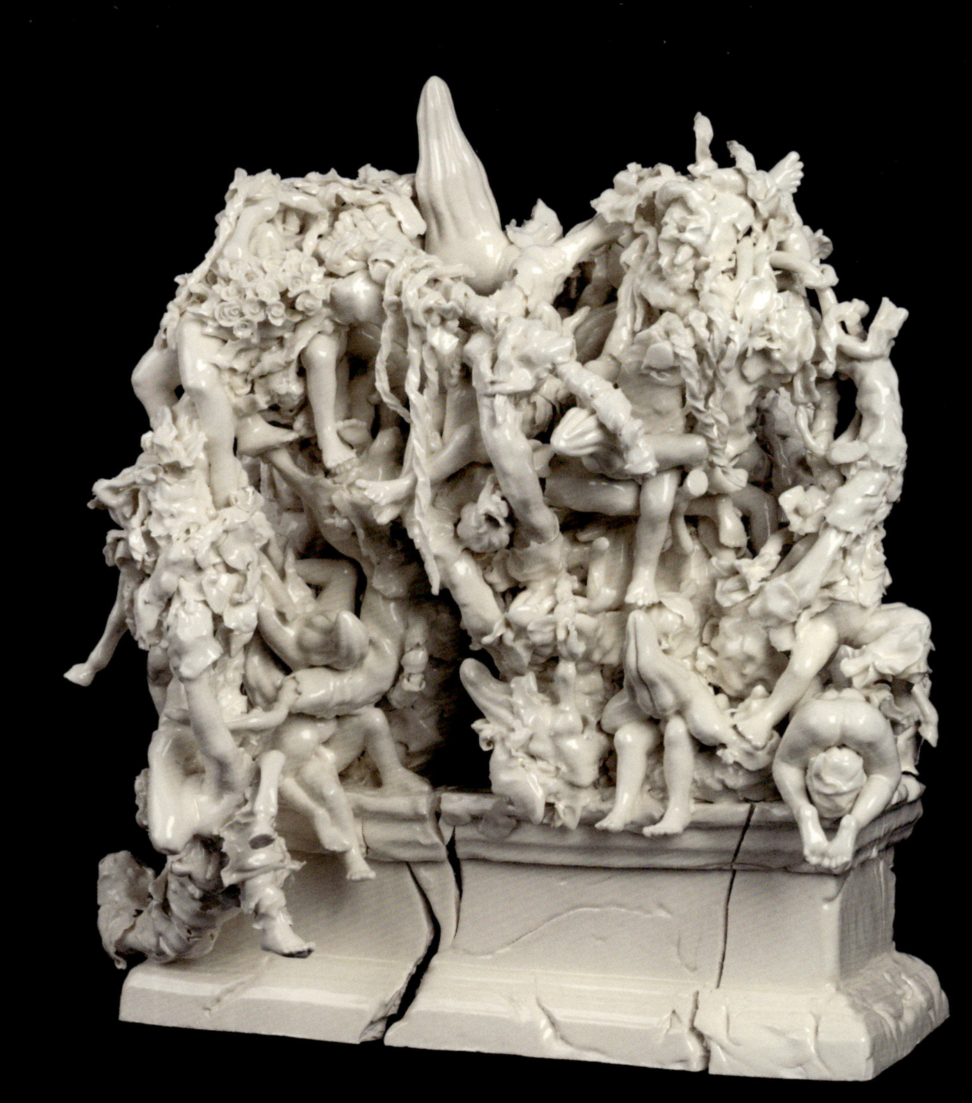

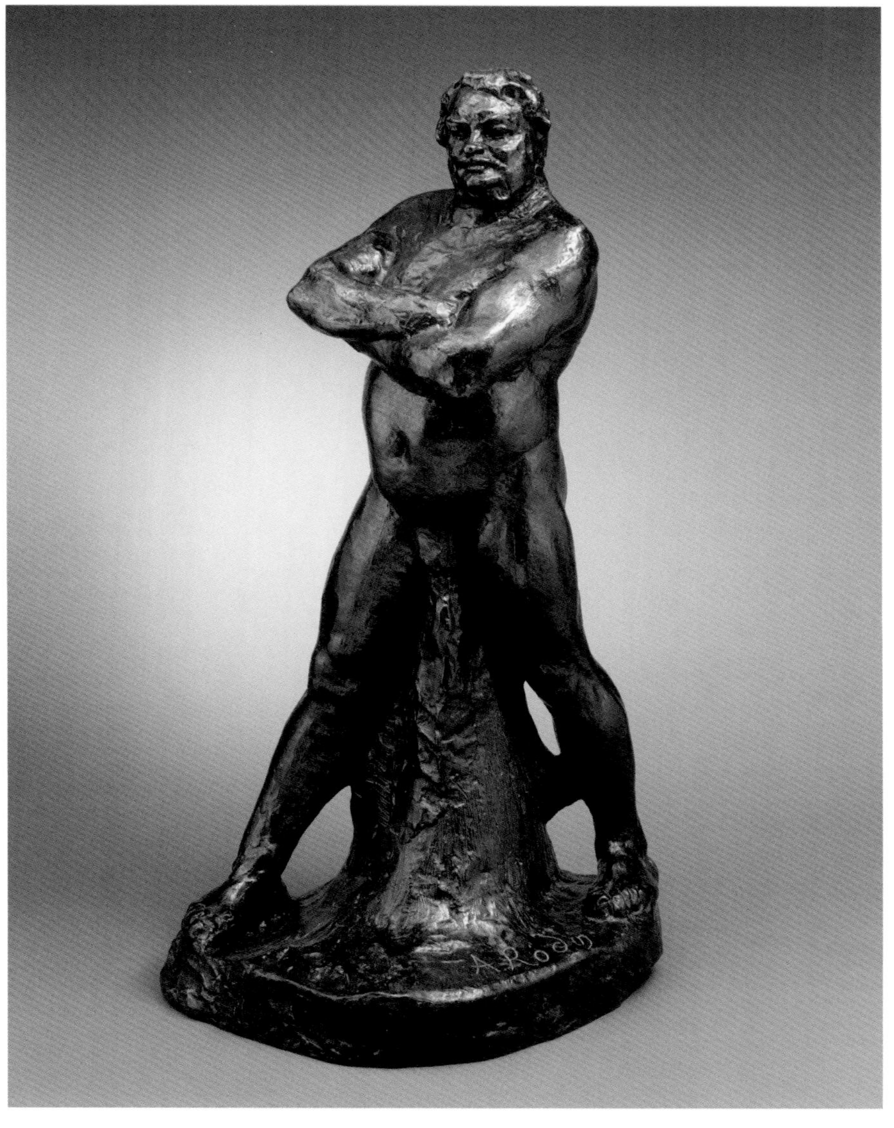

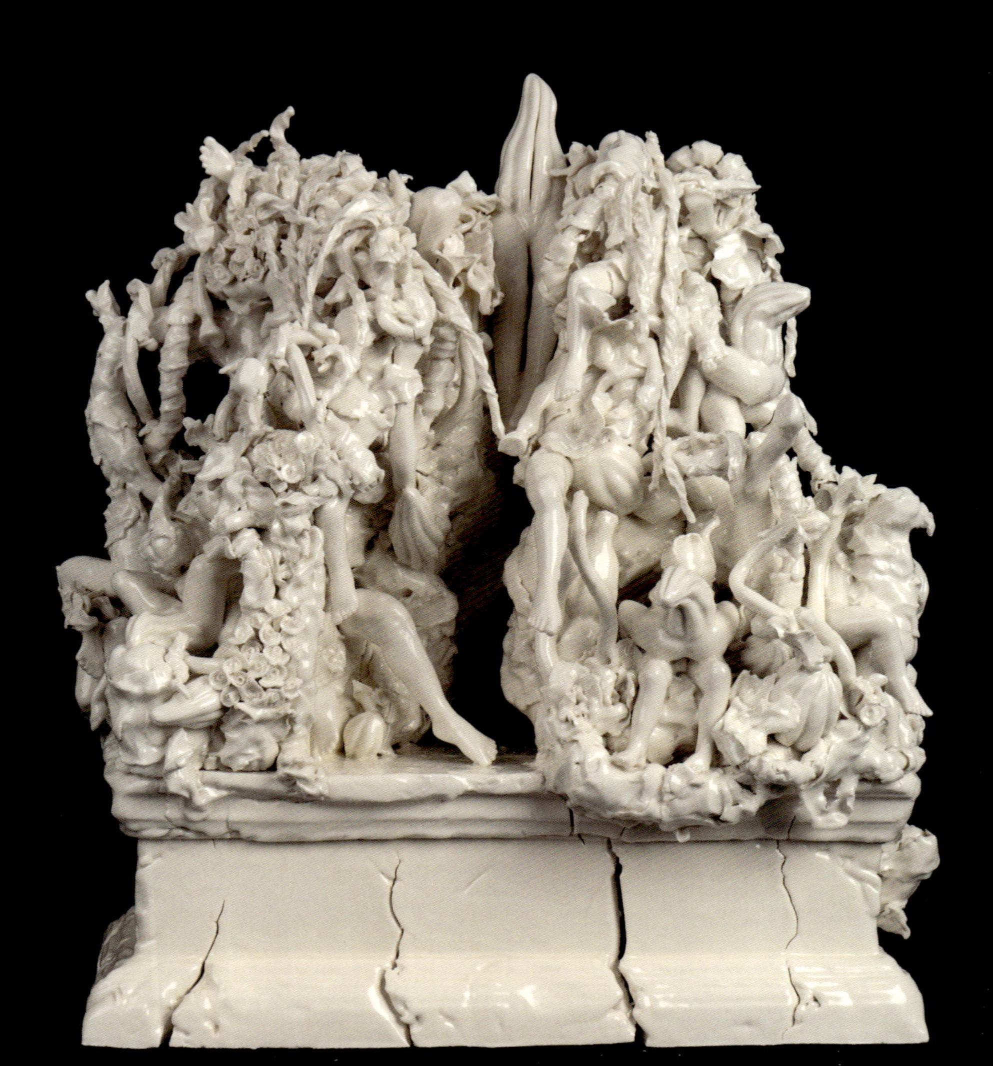

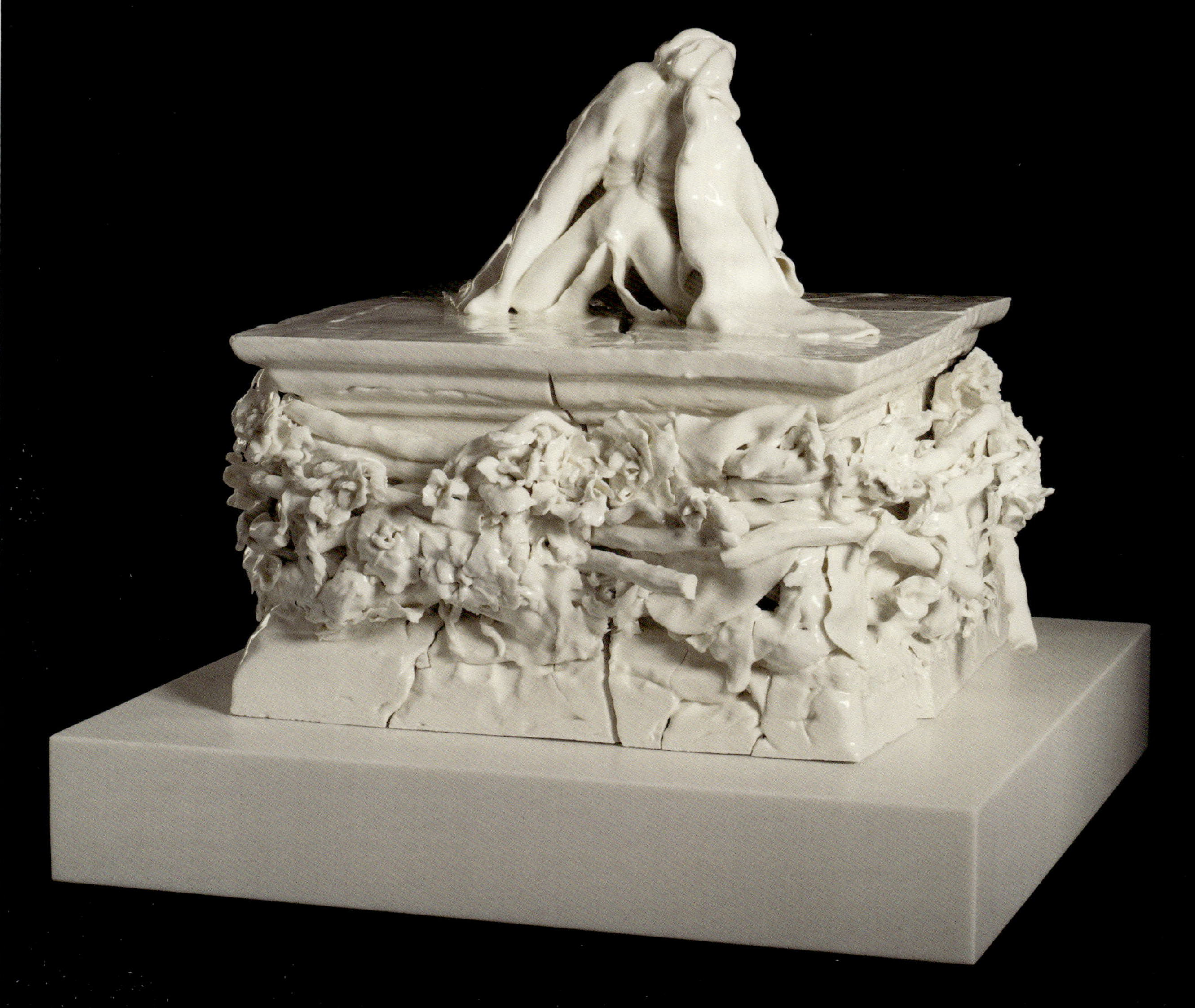

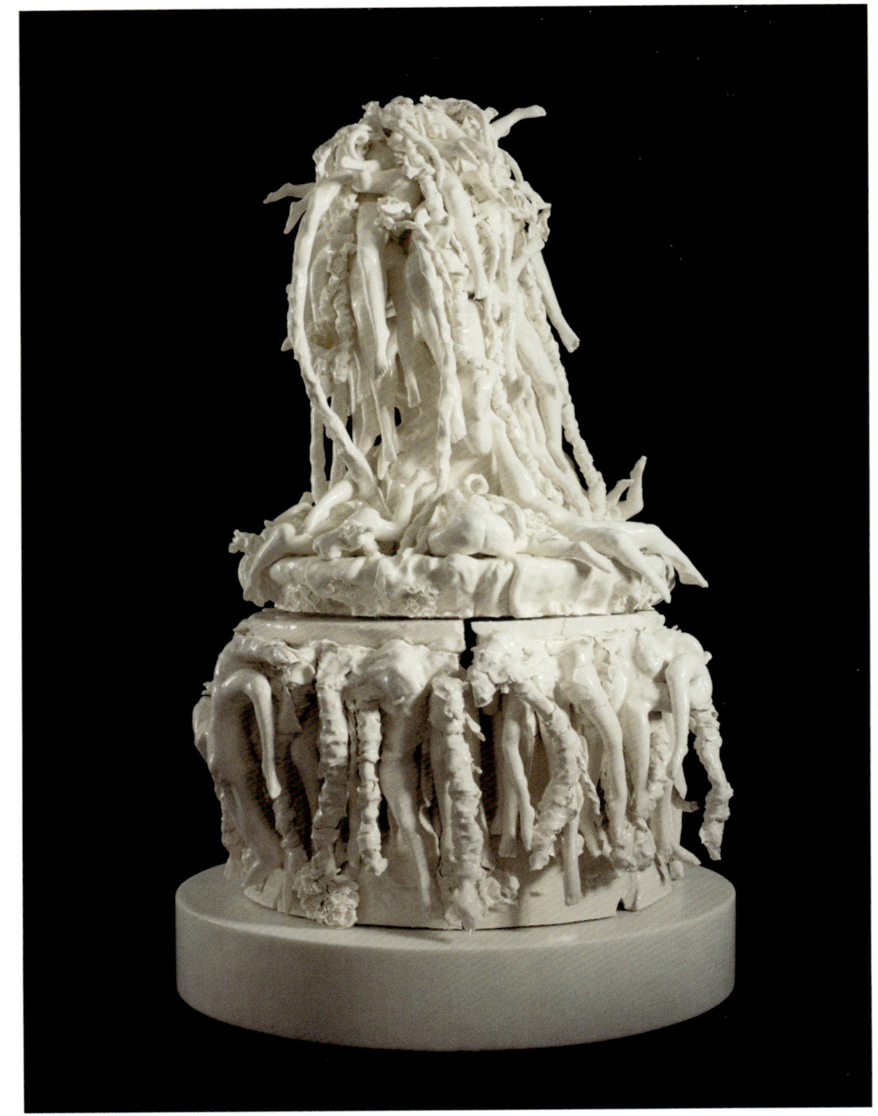

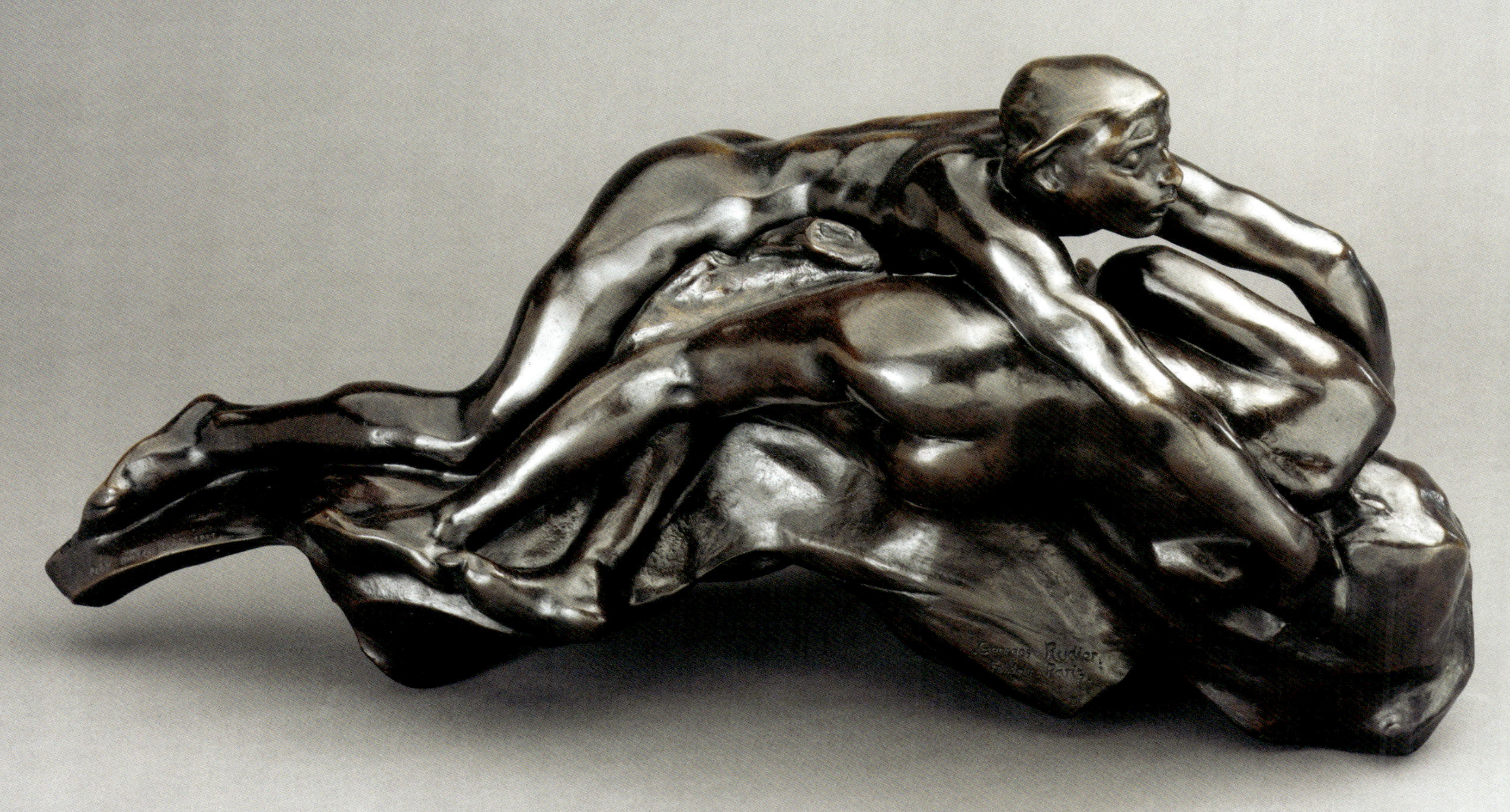

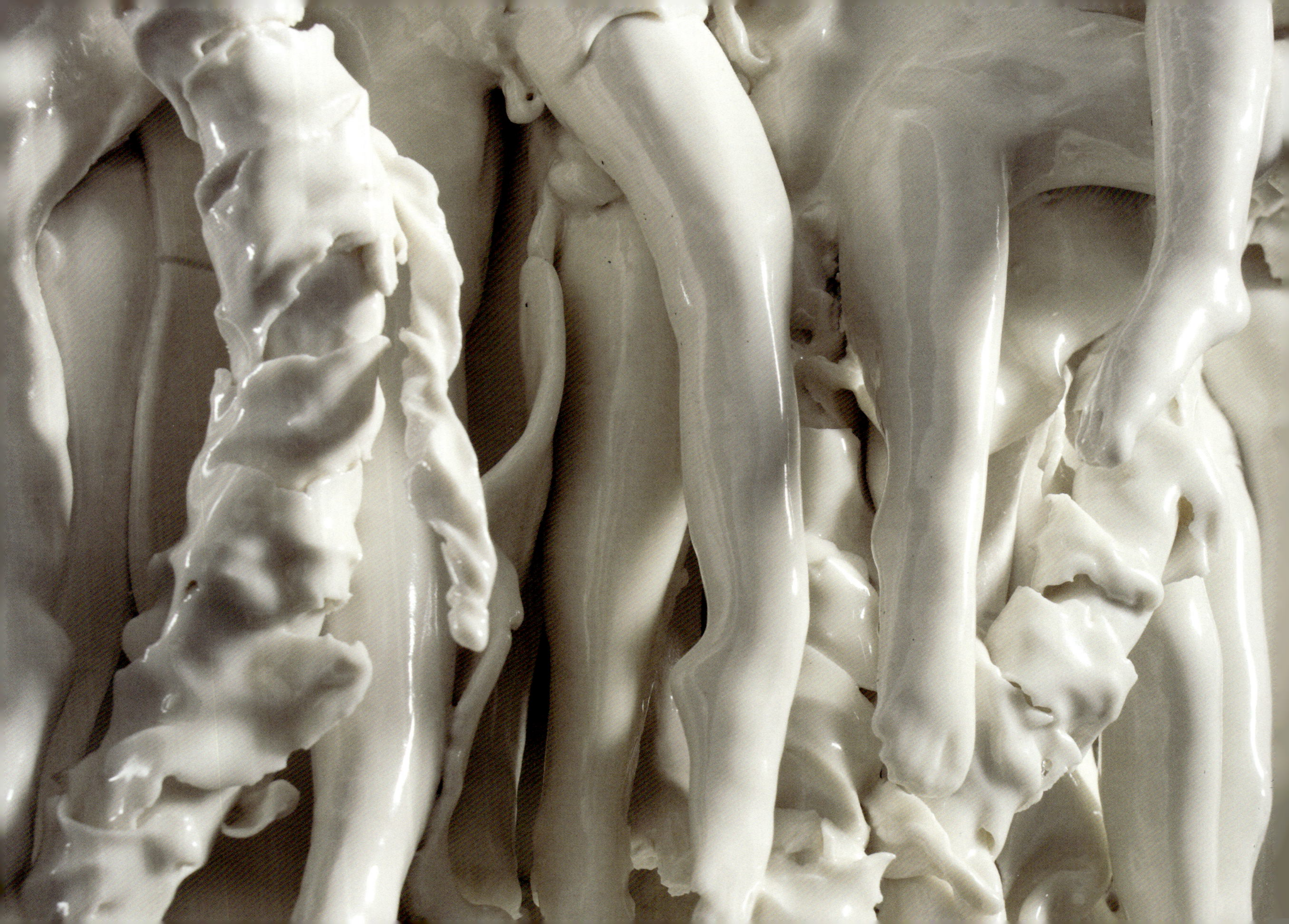

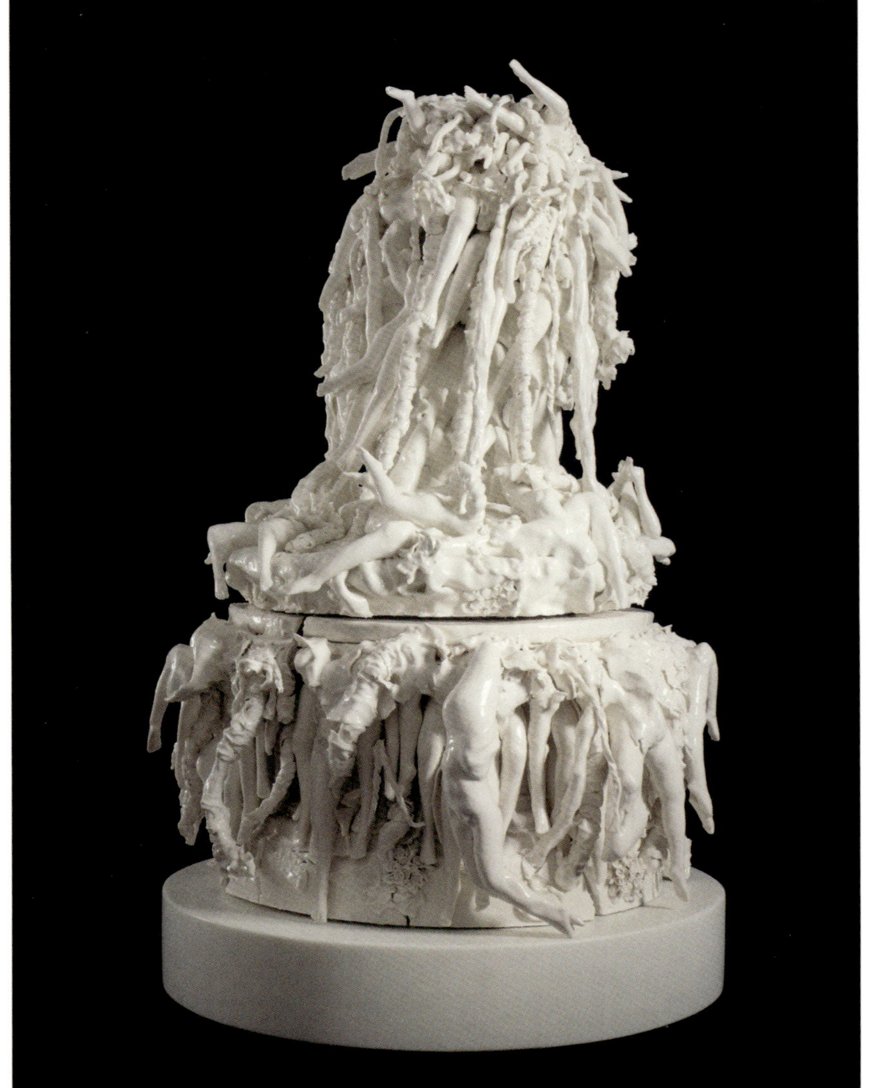

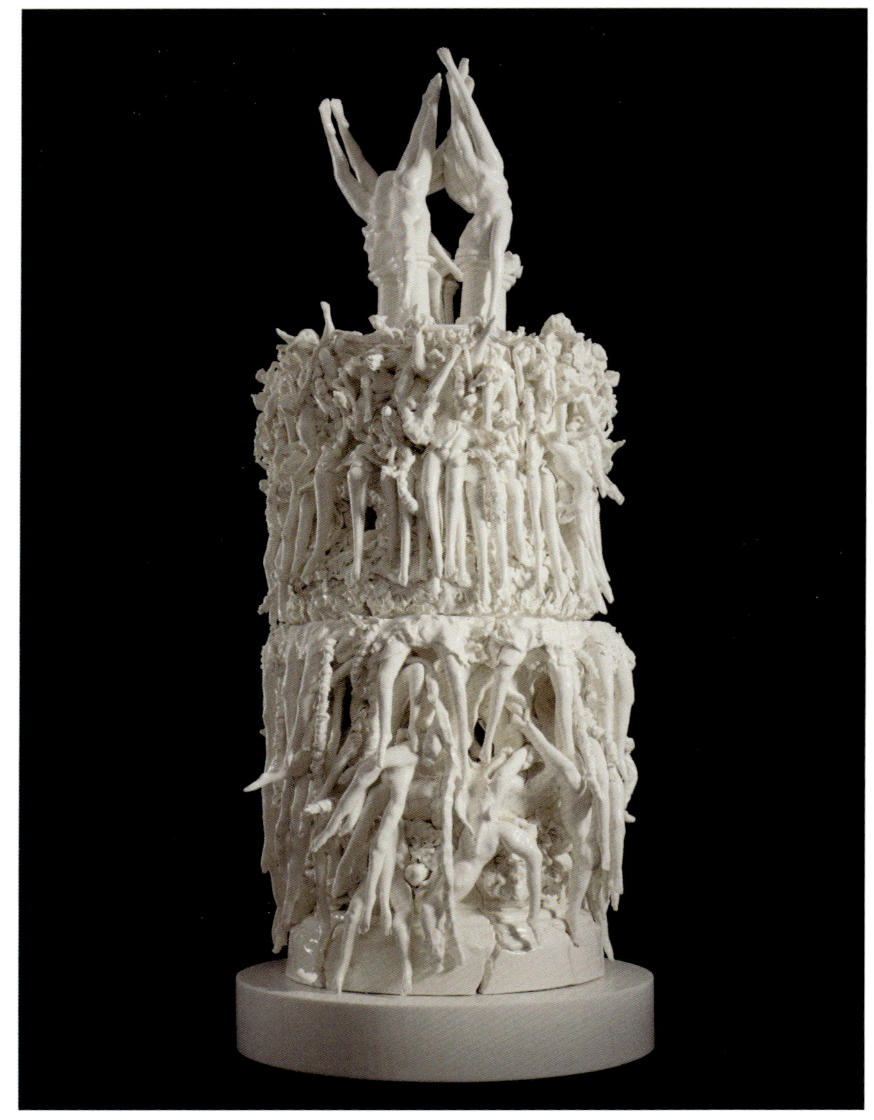

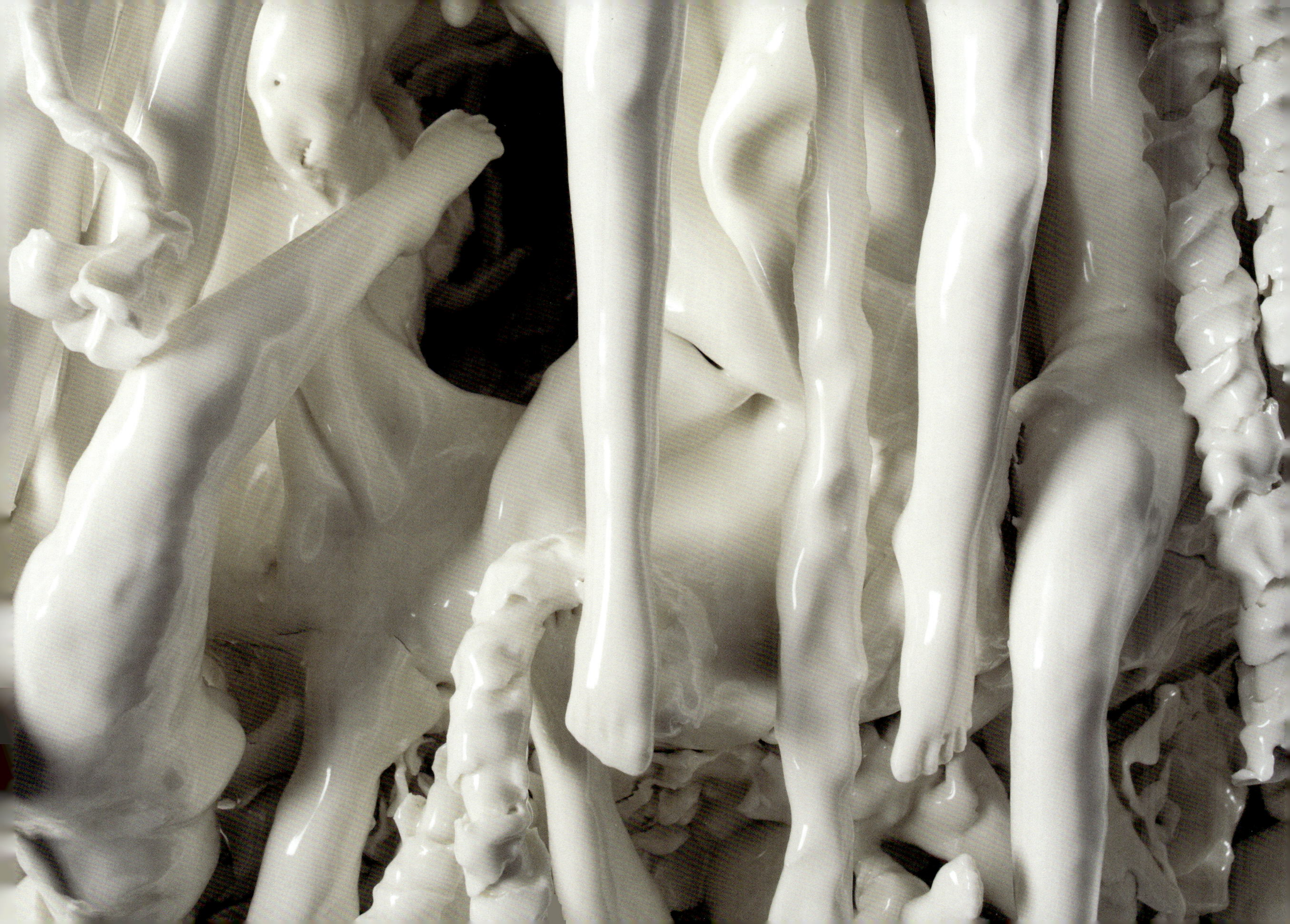

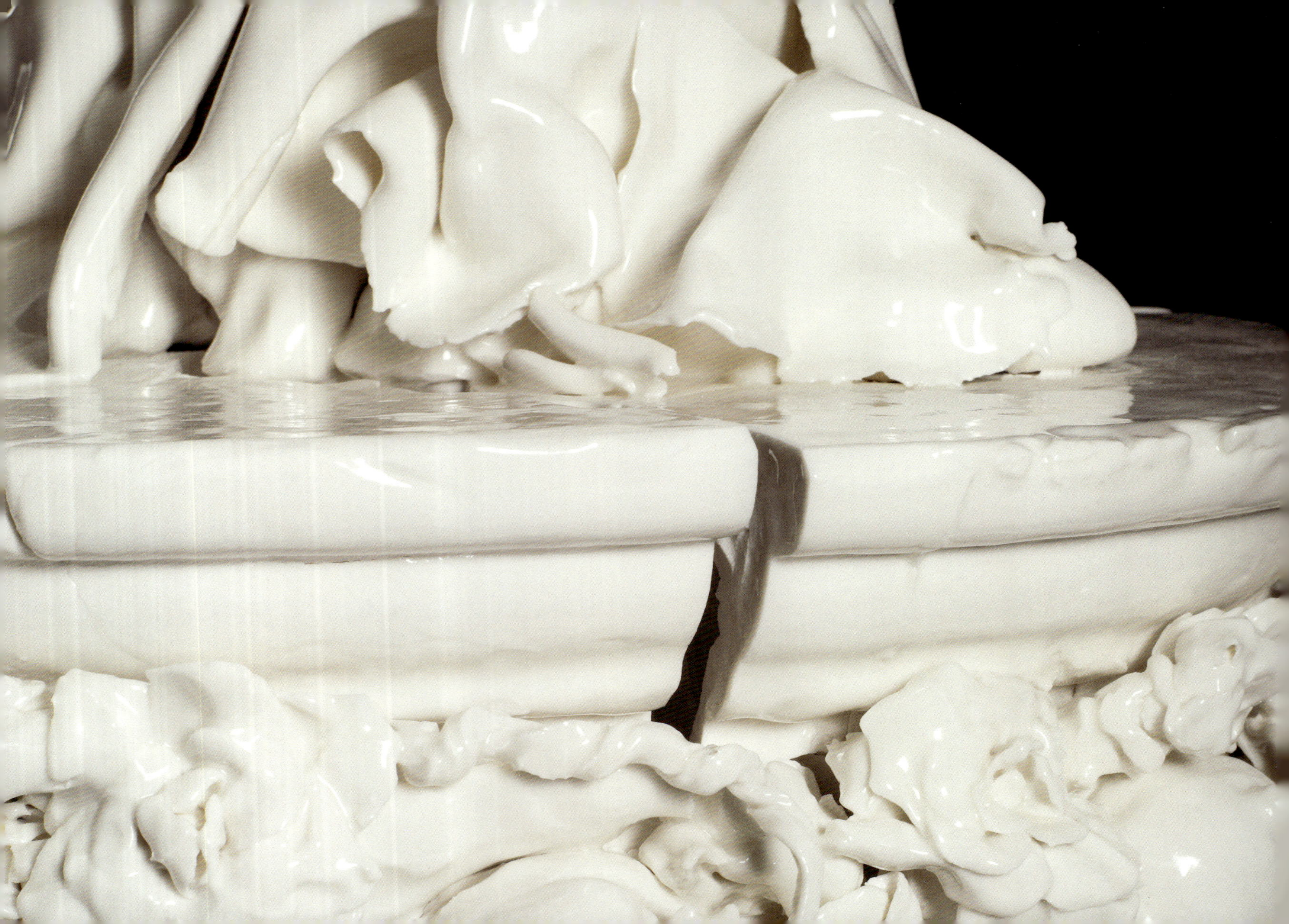

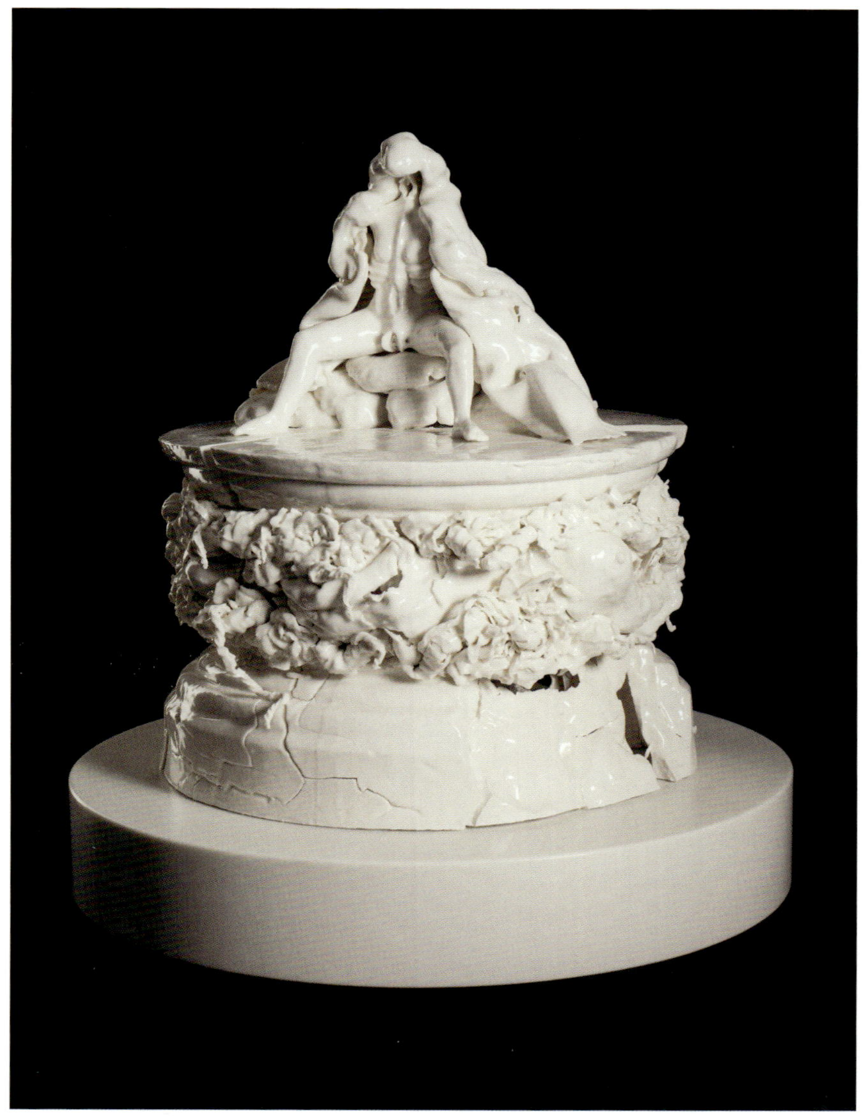

OS

Michelangelo knew the story of Marsyas inside out. A god descends because he hears that a mere mortal being plays his flute as if he's near-divine instead of just another satyr, not even half a man, more like half a beast. The god challenges the satyr to a play-off. He beats him easily; of course he does; he's a god. The prize is the right to skin the satyr alive.

So Apollo, the god, ties Marsyas, the musician, to a tree, nicks him open and peels him whole (this is a story also memorialised in the figure of St Bartholomew, martyred by being flayed alive and consequently the patron saint of tanners, shoe-makers, butchers and skinners, and who, in depictions, usually carries a book and a knife since books used to be bound in skins, and often also carries his own empty skin folded over his arm and even sometimes, unless I'm imagining it, slung rather camply over his shoulder like a jacket).

Poor Marsyas, far too good with his Dionysian flute at playing the tunes of the dark and the ecstatic and the unbridled, has to be brought to order by the scathing Apollonian knife; the half-beast artist has to be tortured so that the god can win his laurels again.

To renaissance eyes it was only proper, and it was a purifying rite.

Marsyas is transformed by the sacrifice: "why do you rip me from myself?" Dante yells at Apollo. "Enter me at the chest, change and fill me with your spirit, do to me what you did to Marsyas when you tore off what covered his body." But there's a more subtle payoff for Marsyas in the exchange. Depending on the version, the climax of this story, which is all about forms of transformation, provides yet another transformation, one which involves an unexpected communality. The crowd of onlookers and bystanders which likes to follow Marsyas about listening to his wild and beautiful tunes, augmented by the even larger crowd drawn by the fun of watching a martyrdom, forms into a mass of witnesses all moved to tears at the skinning of the musician.

They're much more moved by this than by the music played by either satyr or god.

'I' sto rinchiuso come la midolla / da la sua scorza, qua pover e solo, / come spirto legato in un'ampolla' (I am shut in like a marrow by its skin, poor and alone here, like a genie trapped in a bottle.' trans. Christopher Ryan). This is Michelangelo, who conjurs, with these images, the fusion of ecstatic, self-sacrificial and desirous held in the urge to shed the pelt-held lonely self. Whatever comes between us and the world is what traps and separates us, he suggests, implying the waiting wish-fulfilment, the shift from vegetal to magic spirit, even in the mere rubbing-up against whatever's beyond the separateness signalled by skin. In another of his poems, sonnet 94:

O fussi sol la mie l'irsuta pelle
che, del suo pel contesta, fa tal gonna
che con ventura stringe sì bel seno,
ch'i' l'are' pure il giorno; o le pianelle
che fanno a quel di lor basa e colonna,
ch'i' pur ne porterei duo nevi almeno.

('Oh might my skin alone be the hairy skin that, woven from its own skin, makes the gown whose good fortune it is to bind so lovely a breast, so that I should have it at least in the daytime; or might I be the slippers which make themselves a base and support for him, that I might at the very least carry him for two winters.' trans. Christopher Ryan) The speaker in this poem, 'sol per morte si può dir ben nato' (born, it might be said, only in order to die) longs to shed his skin and give himself over so completely not just so that his dead pelt might keep his beloved clothed and warm, but also 'pur per morte potria cangiar mie stato' (so I might, through death, change my state).

Removing the surface between us and the world is a matter of several possible things, then: exceptional art and artistry, earthly needs and aspirations, engagement and response, purification rite, ecstatic abasement, transformation, self-revelation, age-old brand new rebirth, but above all something of the *seek* that naturally goes with all notions of *hide*.

'An endless variety of living surfaces'
(Rilke on Rodin)

Kneebone's work is about brokenness. It's about how to be broken open.

In the making, quite practically, it invites chance and fracture. Its subject is partly the forms that things really do take, in their own process, their own being made.

Its cracks are exciting, extra-sensual textures which demonstrate how to break, how to be broken and yet still stay whole. Her working process allows and makes use of this business of form's independence, its arguing-back, its going its own way. The cracks are form's voice, argument and expression; their fragility is itself a kind of strength of determination because breakage here is implicit, there's air and light and visible dimension because of it in the otherwise solid and weighty, and an intimation of what's seen and what can't be seen, a geology which Kneebone refers to as 'the faultline that isn't a fault.' This geology is raucous and grave, a matter of both intimacy and theatricality. It's fixed and fluid both, jagged and smooth both, pure and rotten both, broken and whole both. It's as white as a wedding cake, but a wedding cake that breaks itself open on its way to its own ritual so as to defy any attempt at mere promise. This is an active art.

*'The language of this art was the body ... it had become
a different body'*
(Rilke on Rodin)

When does soft become hard become clay become porcelain become petal? When does petal become knife? When did flowers get an edge that would split skin open? The work here slices clean through, like they were ripe fruit, both the intimate and the historical. Delicacy becomes a rope. The phallus efflorates and becomes vulva. The penile in a DNA twist grows a whorl of roses whose petals will make you bleed. Genitals are mouths and bodies end in tongues, they end in clitoral fruited forms both simultaneously phallic and vulvic. Their folds are labial and stiff. Their orgiastics are fearful, liberating, profoundly erotic and eroticised both. The revelation is that nothing's not related, mud and worm and tendril and bloom, yielding and fishy and hellish and beautiful and as efflorescent and full of life as any Botticelli, as grave as any tomb.

> *'There is a weeping of the whole body ... the suffering*
> *bodies of another generation'*
> (Rilke on Rodin)

Viewing Kneebone's work is like witnessing the centuries in gracious hellish meltdown.

To view it is to experience, embodied and direct, an encounter with something smouldering and pure both at once.

The titles she gives her works nick little bits of skin off the expressions of other, often literary, works. They gesture to a fusion of her own work and literature as related forms of expression. They also work their own Calvino magic, where, placed beside each other, they make their own new poem. They refer silently to voice forms. Their fracture, which is all about dimension and stratification, permission and truthfulness, is choral.

> *'A thousand forms of expression for all that was new and nameless*
> *in its development, and for all those ancient secrets'*
> (Rilke on Rodin)

Blake and Dante and Rilke and Rodin and Baudelaire and Michelangelo and Bernini and –

Imagine Rodin took a lover, and –

No, imagine a lover took Rodin and flung him flat against a surface, broke him and watched him reform, stretched him to a new and crucially communal shape. Kneebone's eye plays on all the traditionals and the canonicals with a nonchalance, a knowledge, a century later's wide-open freedom, like when the dancer Michael Clark upended the notion of ballet to reveal at last the bare arse of the classical. There are legs everywhere in the work, a Greek chorus of legs, the chorus, the original Greek dancers, being the original touch-point between the drama and its spectators.

Put Kneebone alongside Rodin:

Freud meets historical holocaust;
time opens to its own future;
the inner self emerges anew again;
the outer self strips back and off between them both like so much old pelt.

The self inside the self outside the self: it's a renaissance unveiling.

*'Nature herself ... traverses silently and seriously the long
pathway to abundance'*
(Rilke on Rodin)

Renaissance veiling and unveiling are in essence the same thing, and are always
about knowledge and power, and for protection from these, proper recognition of
these and help with an understanding of their natures. Kneebone's work, revealing
the attraction, the seriousness and terrifyingness of desire in the primal self, traverses
fish and flower and coral, the bacterial and the genetic and the slime and the mud
and the clay and the form and the bones and the spines, and teems with the deaths
of all these, yes, but most with the life, being so close to an understanding of the
place of small deaths, where blind orgasm becomes its own seeing and each death
meets and releases its opposite.

This is Lacan, on the breakage in lifeforce, the thing that breaks free and "flies off"
when 'the membranes of the egg in which the foetus emerges on its way to becoming

a new-born are broken': 'it is the libido, qua pure life instinct, that is to say, immortal life, or irrepressible life, life that has need of no organ, simplified, indestructible life.'

'It was henceforth a question of making Life'
(Rilke on Rodin)

Am I the only person who sees past the dark, the classical desolation that critics like to see in Kneebone's work? It seems to me to be a refutal of despair, with all the terribleness of beauty, yes, but with a promise of endless expression. And it's meaty. It's forceful. I know it's hell. But it's a hell full of Tiller girls, a place laced with every music hall or follies dancer who ever kicked a leg, every labial frill and thrill, and there are legs everywhere, hoofers via the undeniable thrust and panache of an artist who remakes the graces as disgraces and is wise to the giving and receiving and giving again as being that fiercely, that blindly, that destructively and that creatively physical a part of our (and our planet's) being.

Even in the finalities of history's or fantasy's ghastlinesses, even in prehistory's primordial slime – the kick of this lifeforce. Its liberation from personality is very sexy. I'm almost tempted to call it cheerful because, descent and all, it's a striving upwards, a process in which being broken, losing the self and gaining the anonymity, is not just accepted but garlanded, celebrated, understood in an orgiastic, muscular and vital expression in which Eros and Thanatos are joined at the classical os, or the bone (or the Kneebone), the Greek meets the Latin and the *os* does me the favour of being both bone and mouth, *os, ossa / os, ora* (the former a bone, the latter a mouthlike structure or opening).

> *'Each part was a mouth uttering in its own manner'*
> (Rilke on Rodin)

Kneebone's wide open work is the opposite of arrogance – not humble, or self-effacing, just selfless, plainly present, no posture, no bravado. It is not about attitude. It is art as its own utterance – its own throw – and a celebration of fracture in the ejaculation, a revelation in the act of the art, for which it's worth the shedding of all our self-protection.

Ali Smith

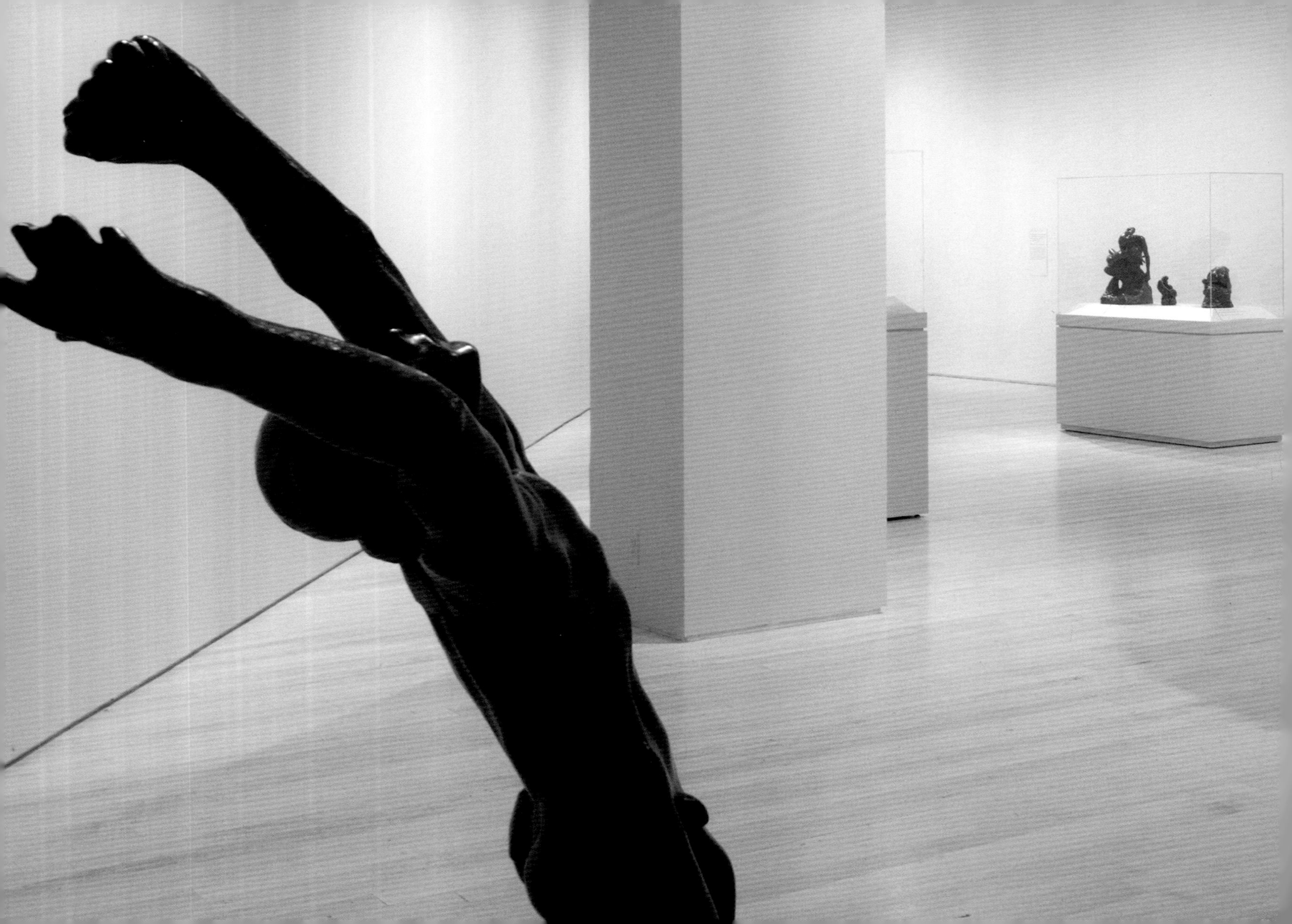

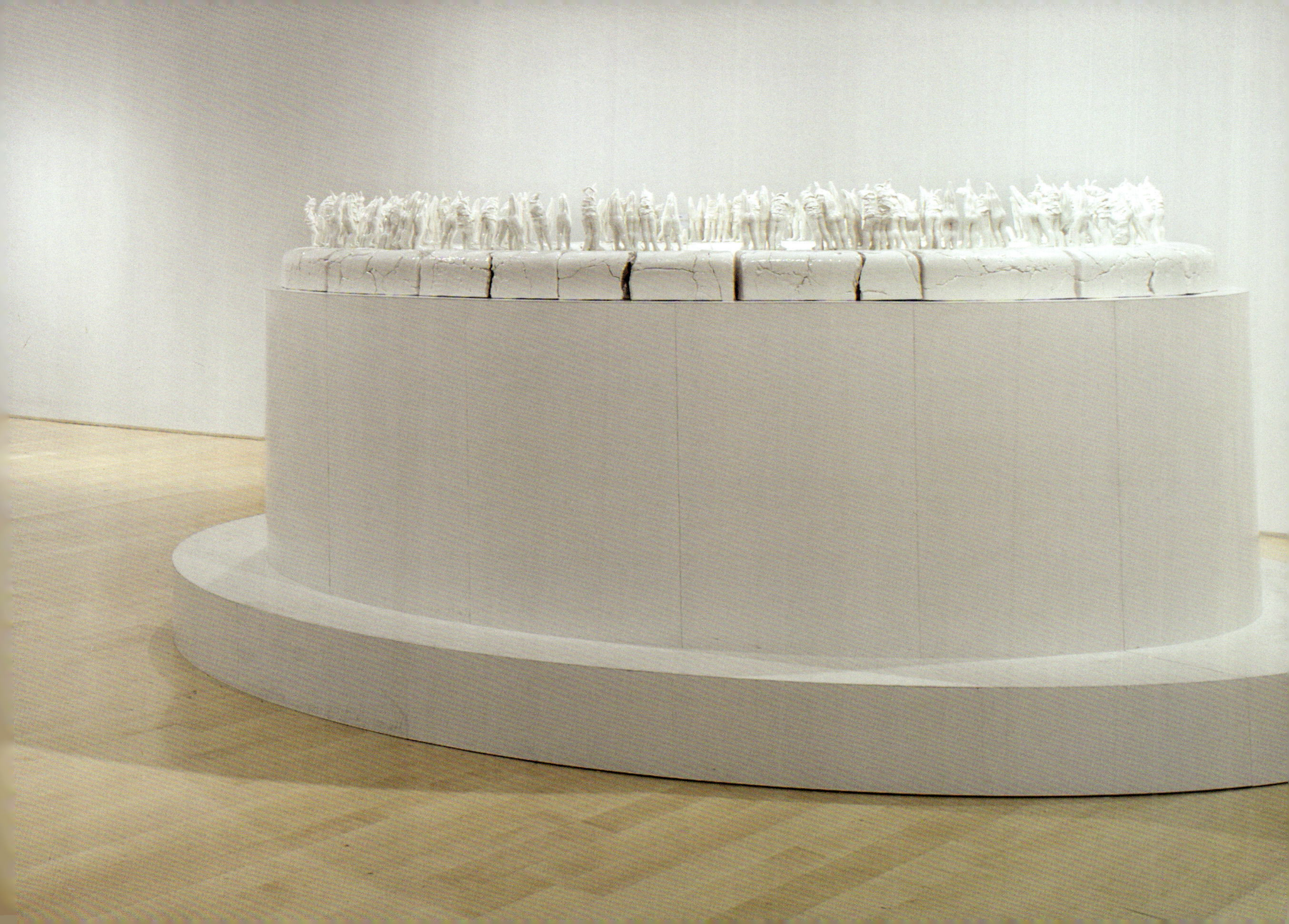

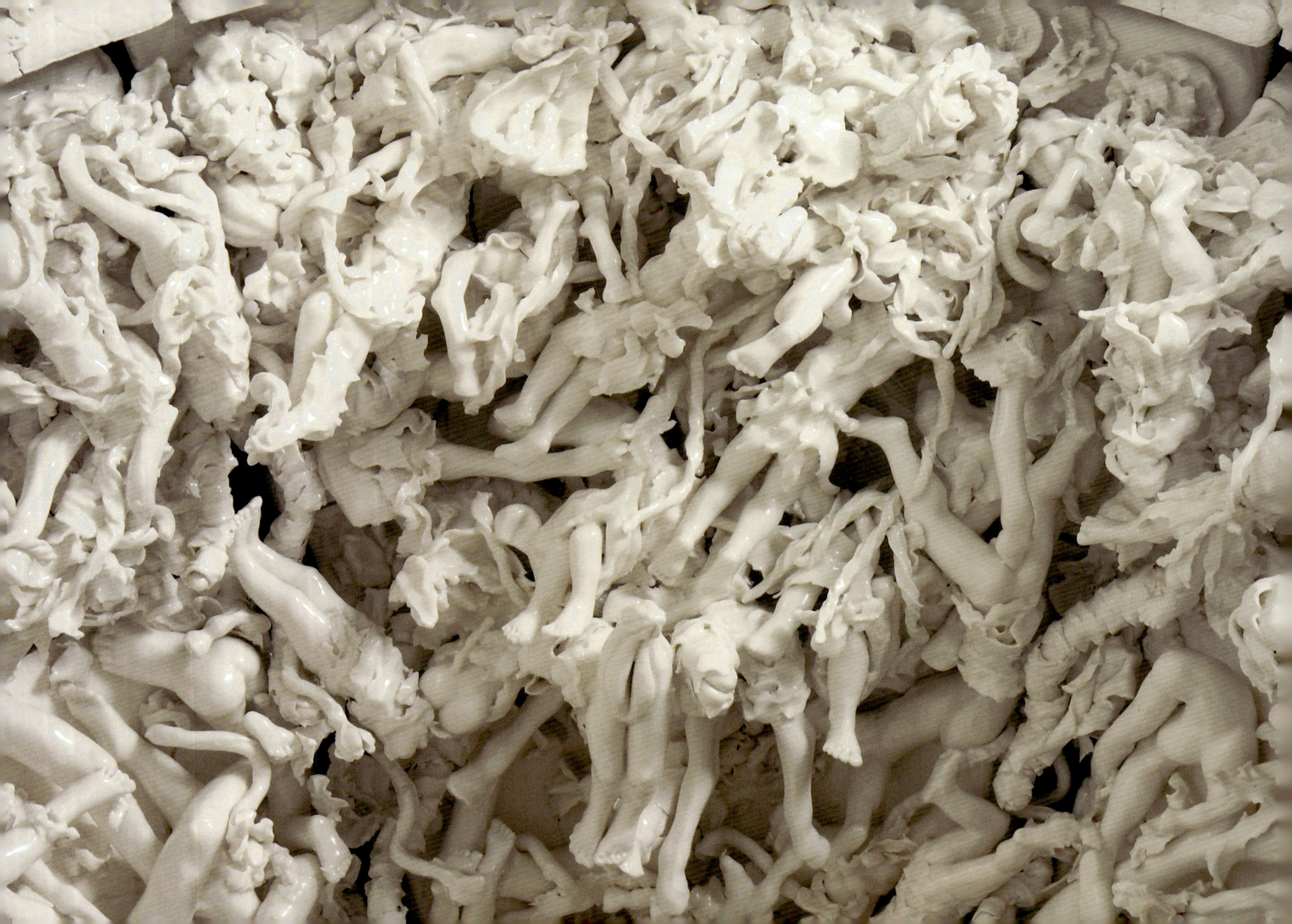

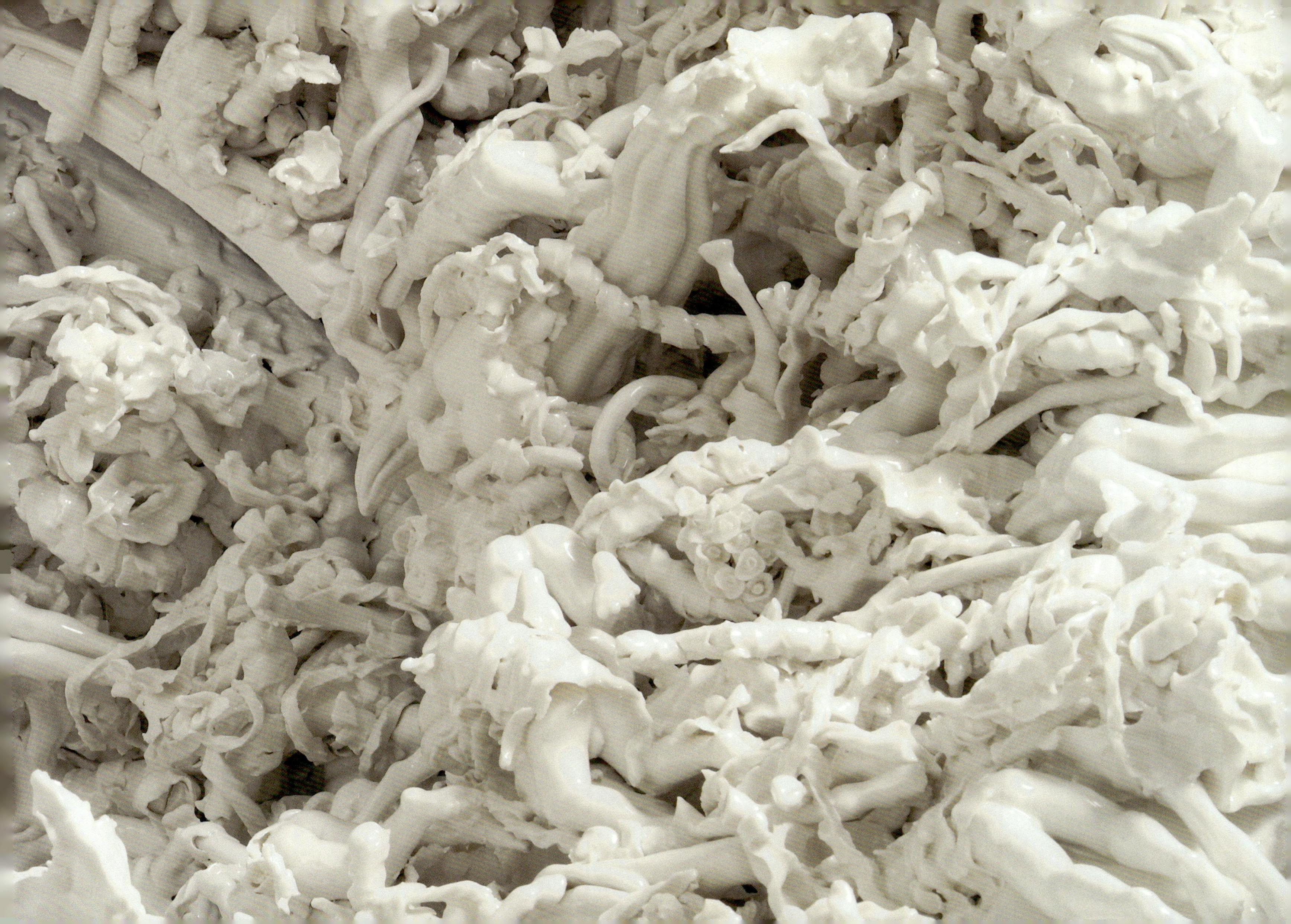

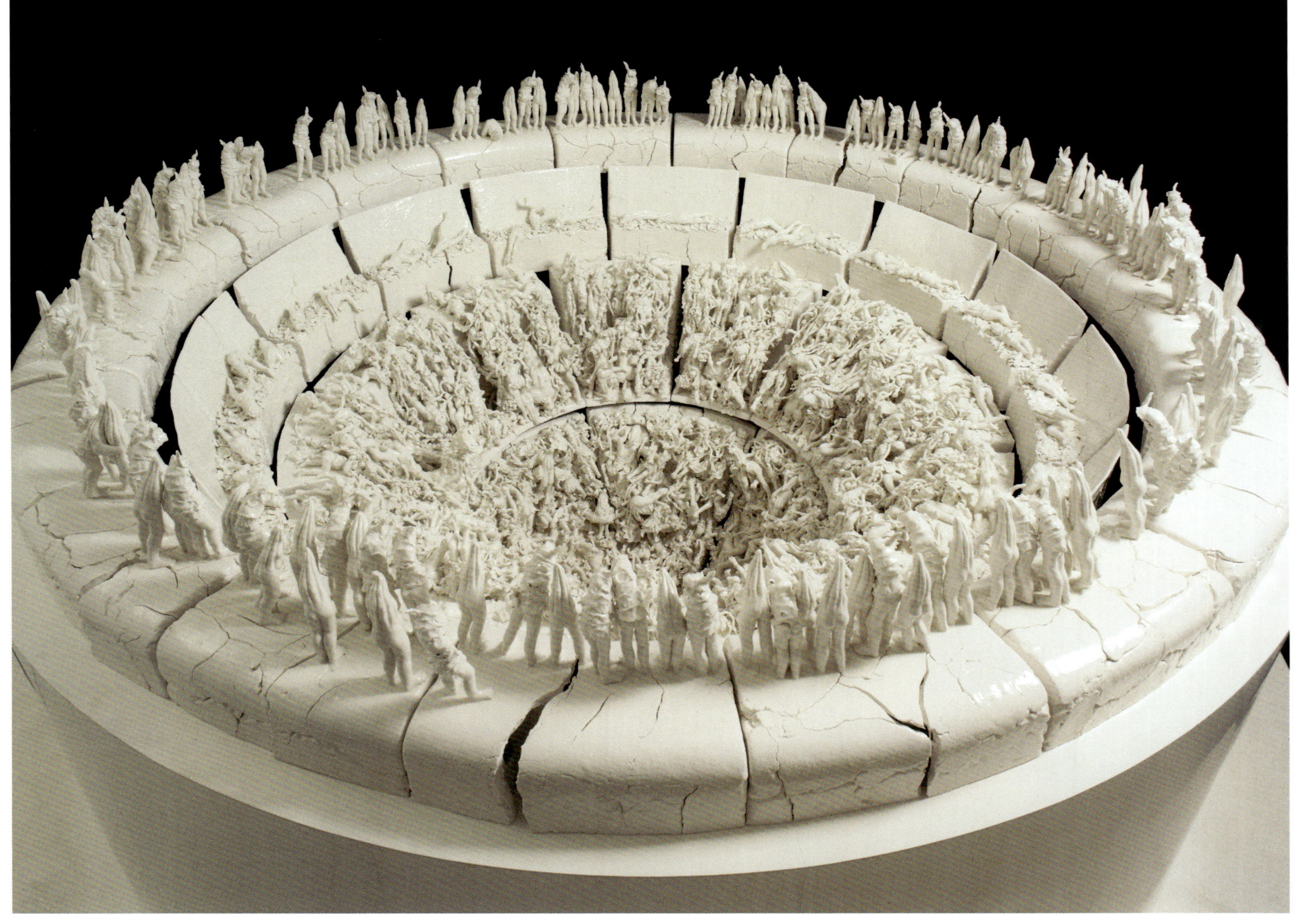

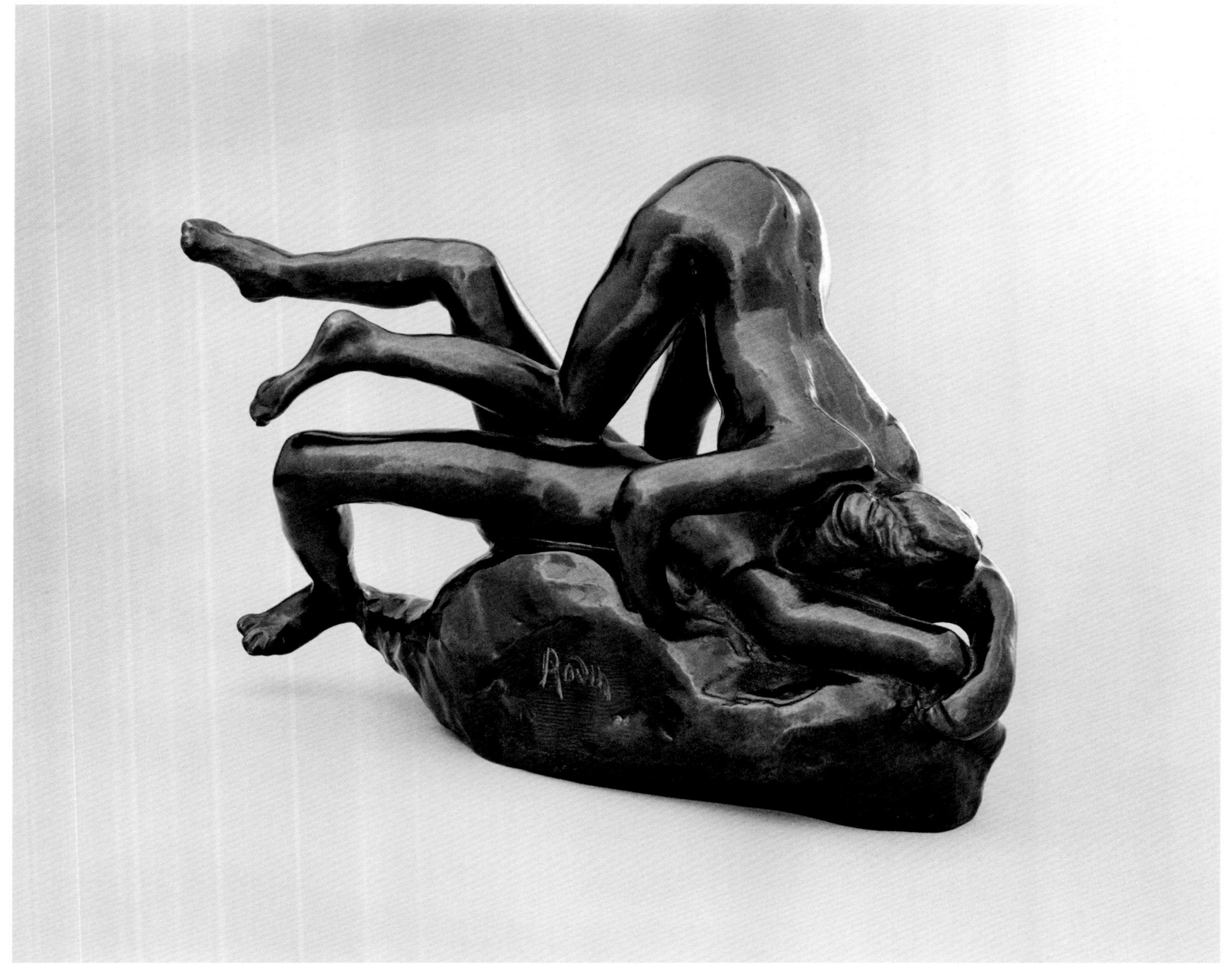

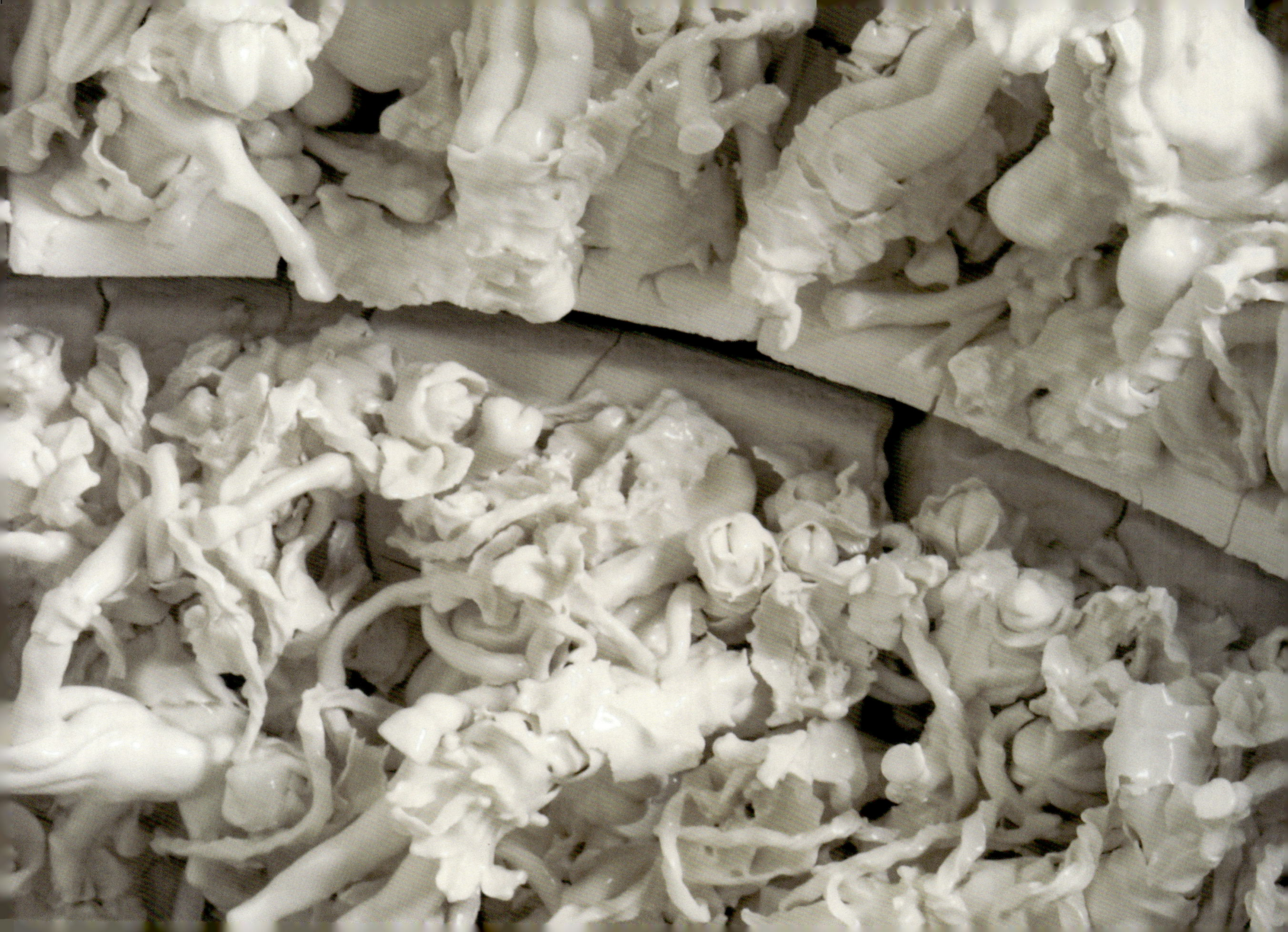

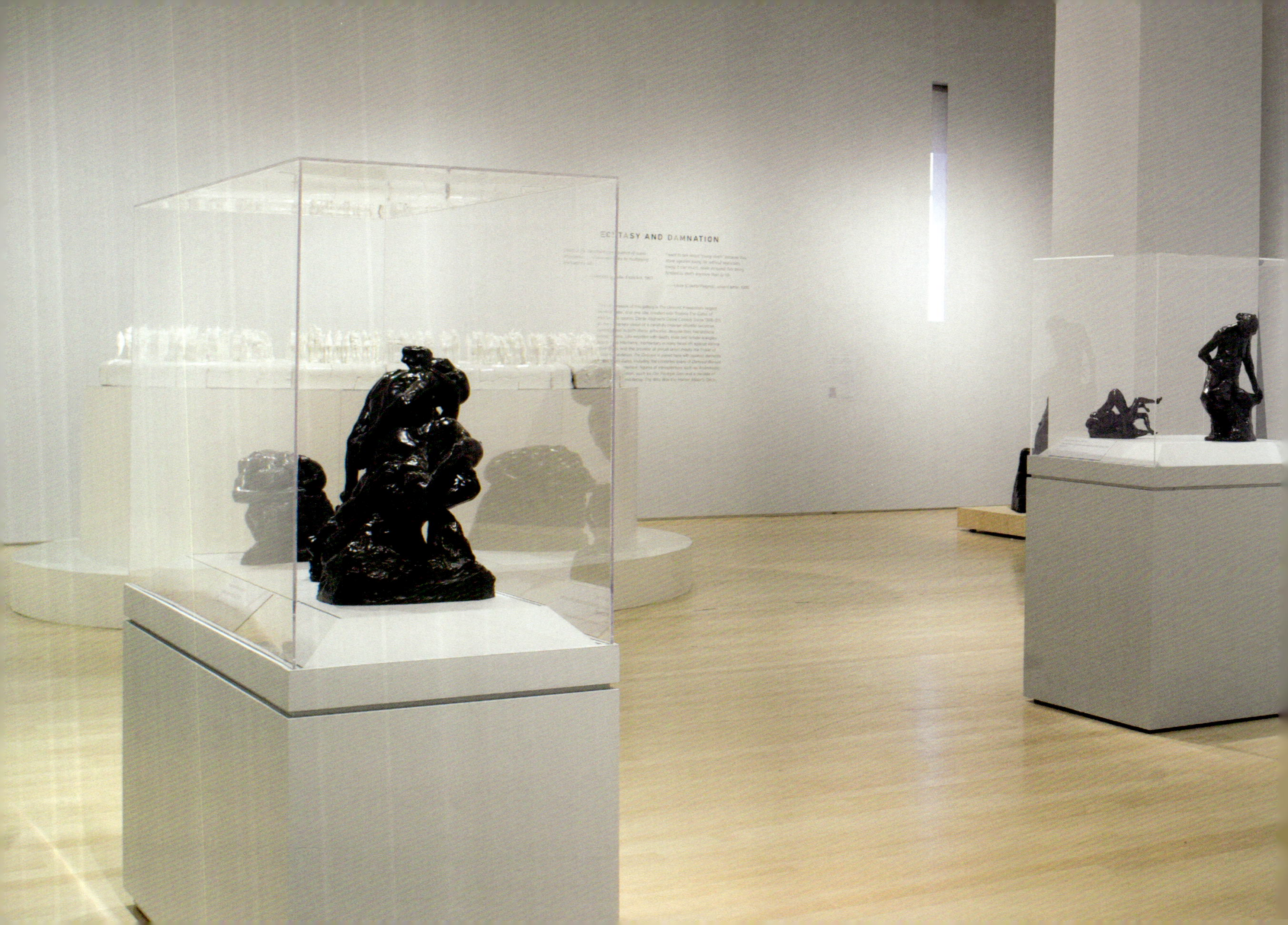

ECSTASY AND DAMNATION

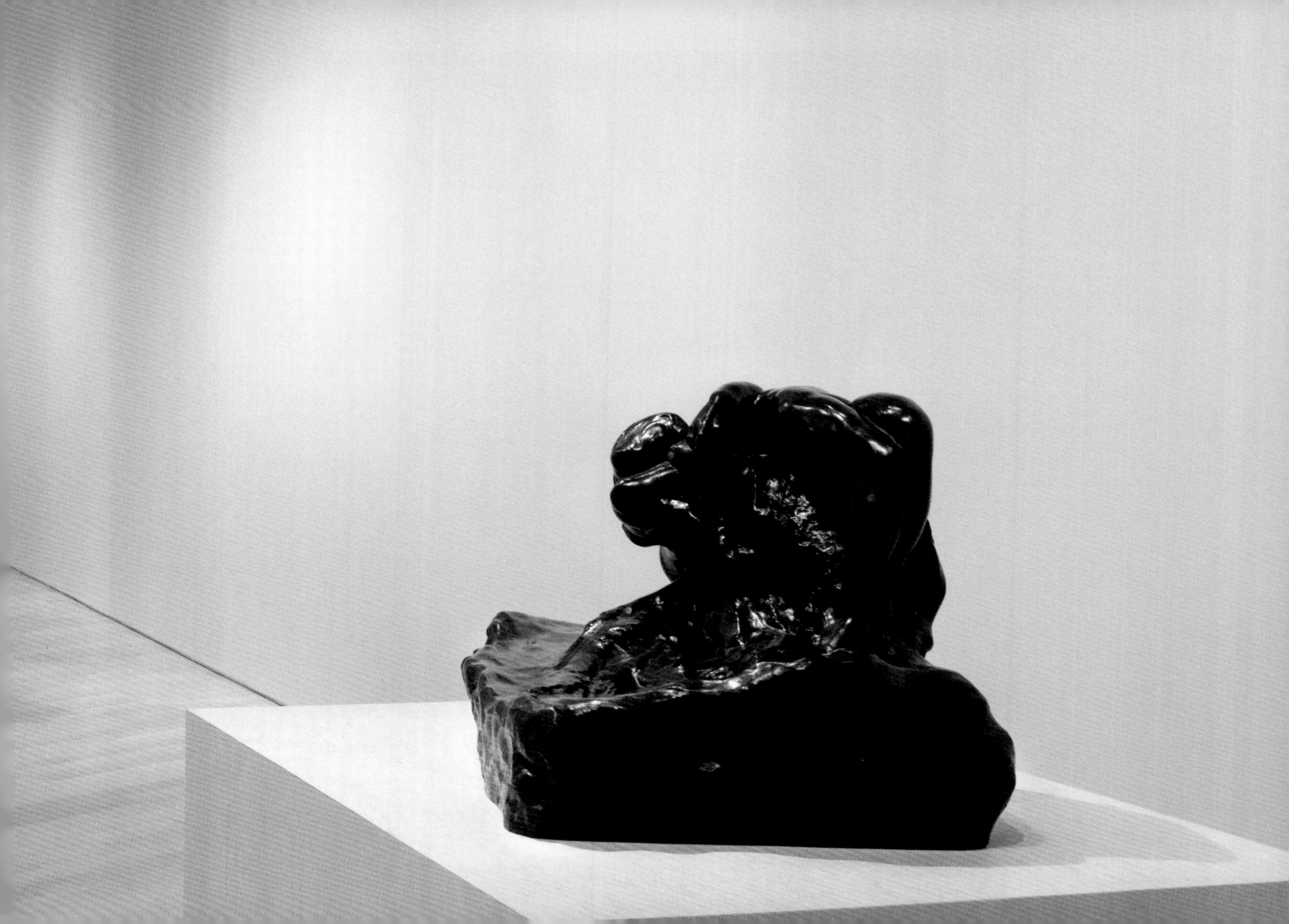

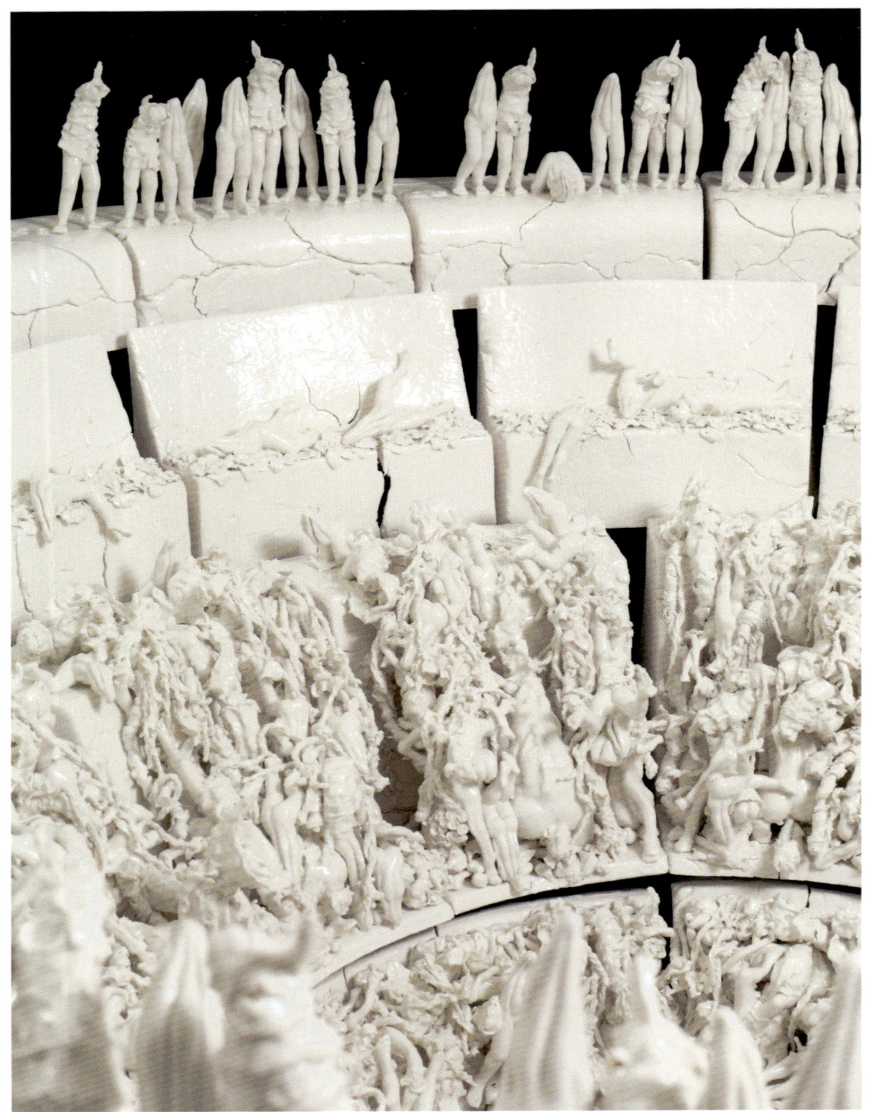

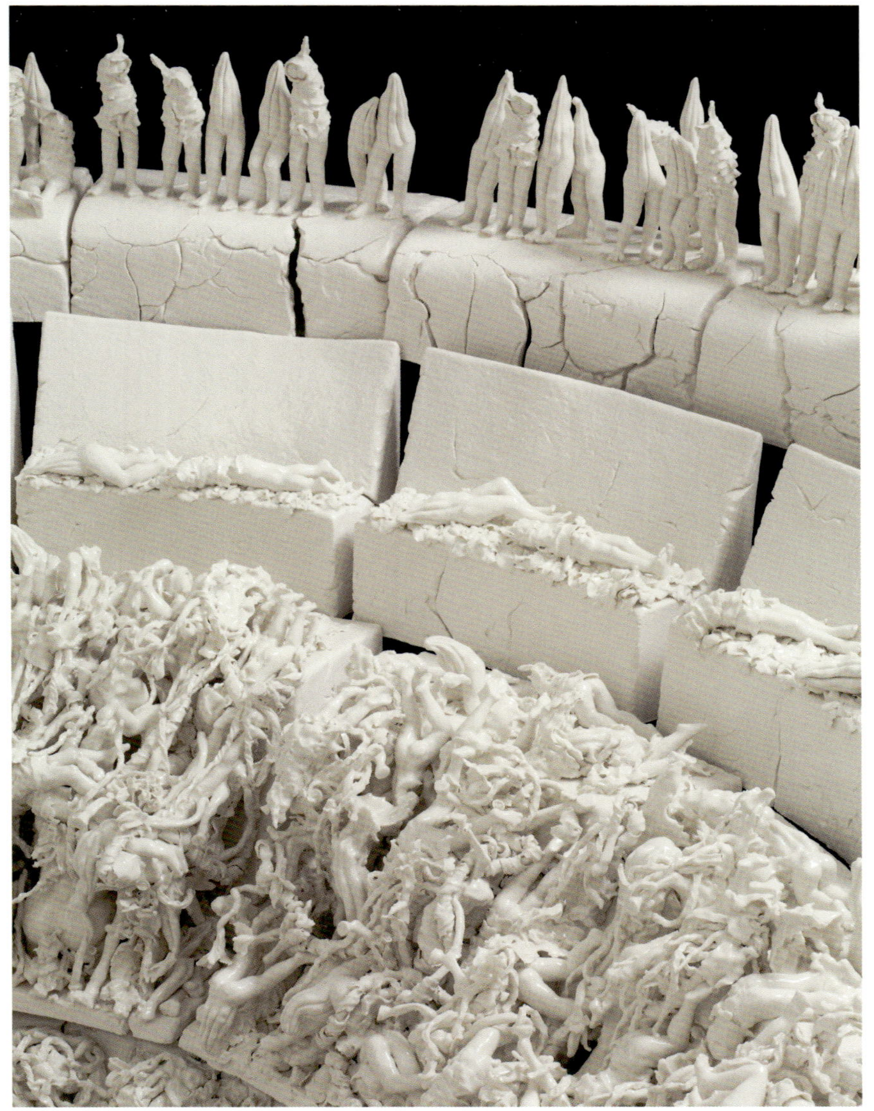

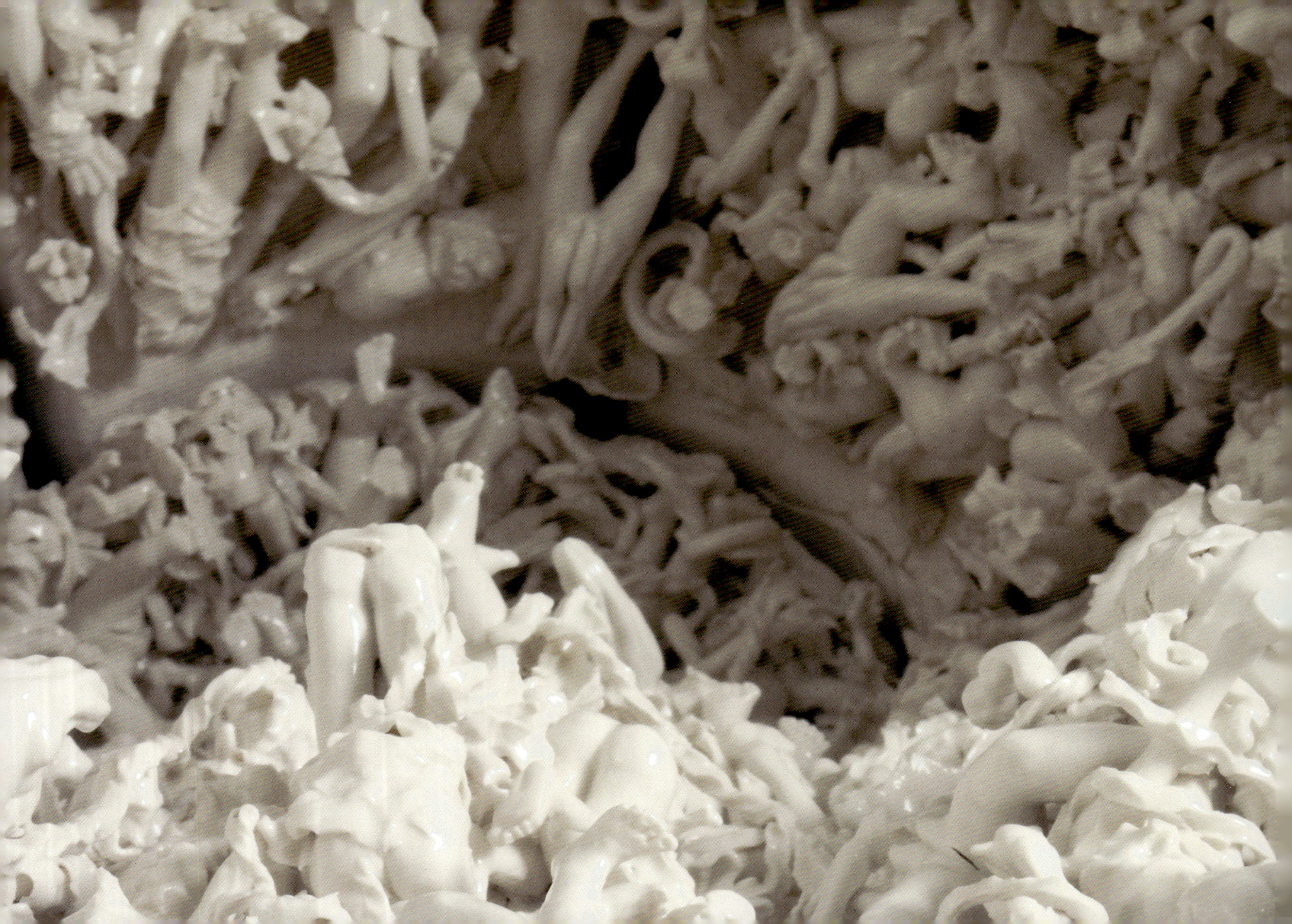

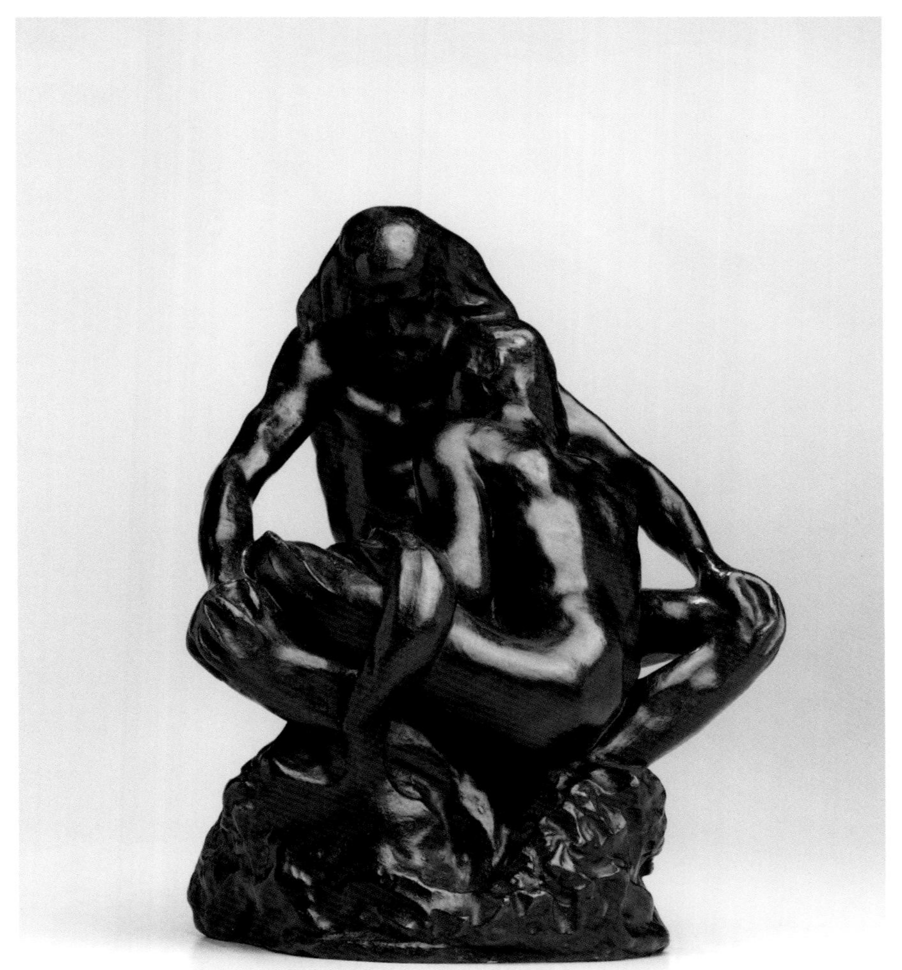

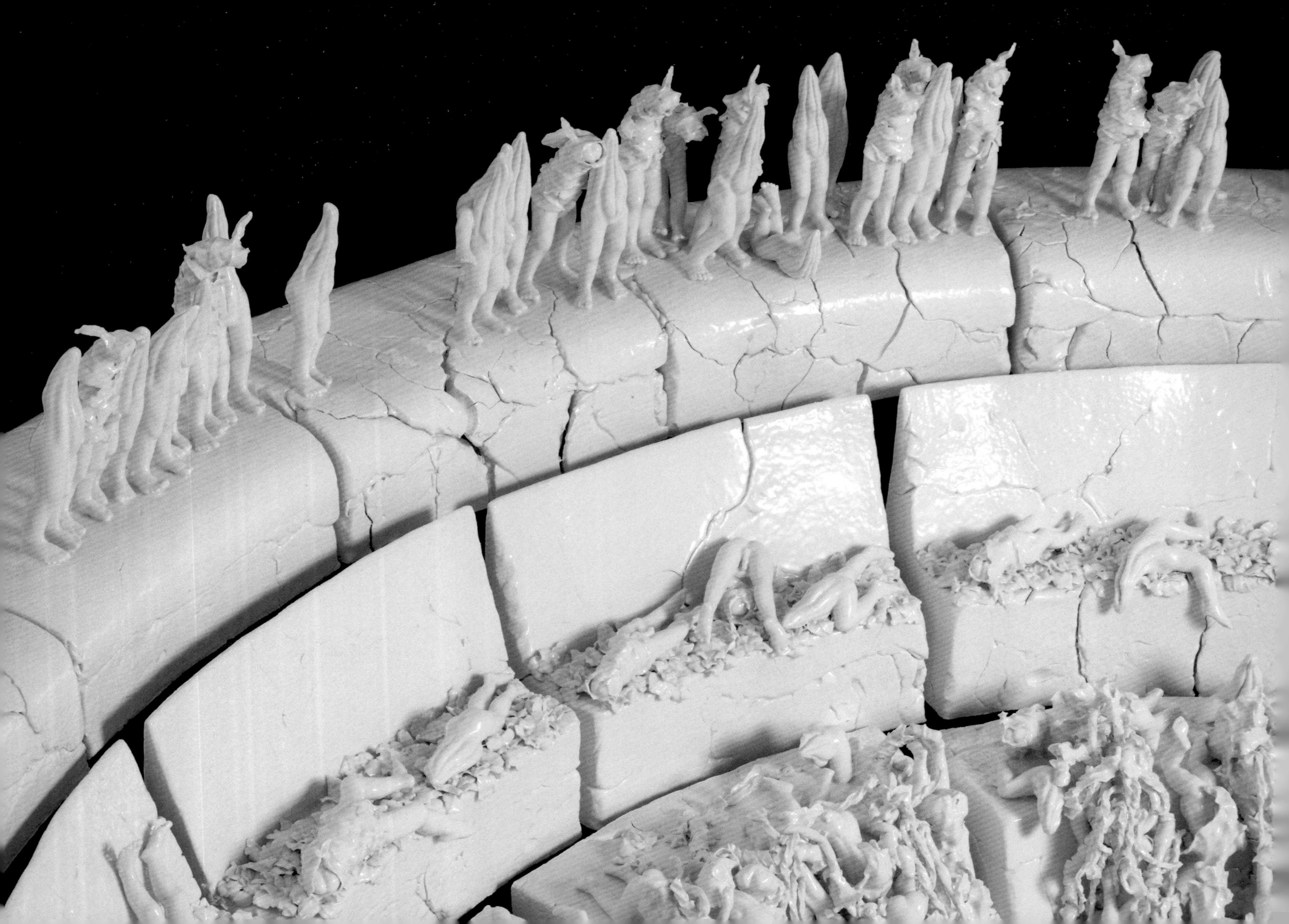

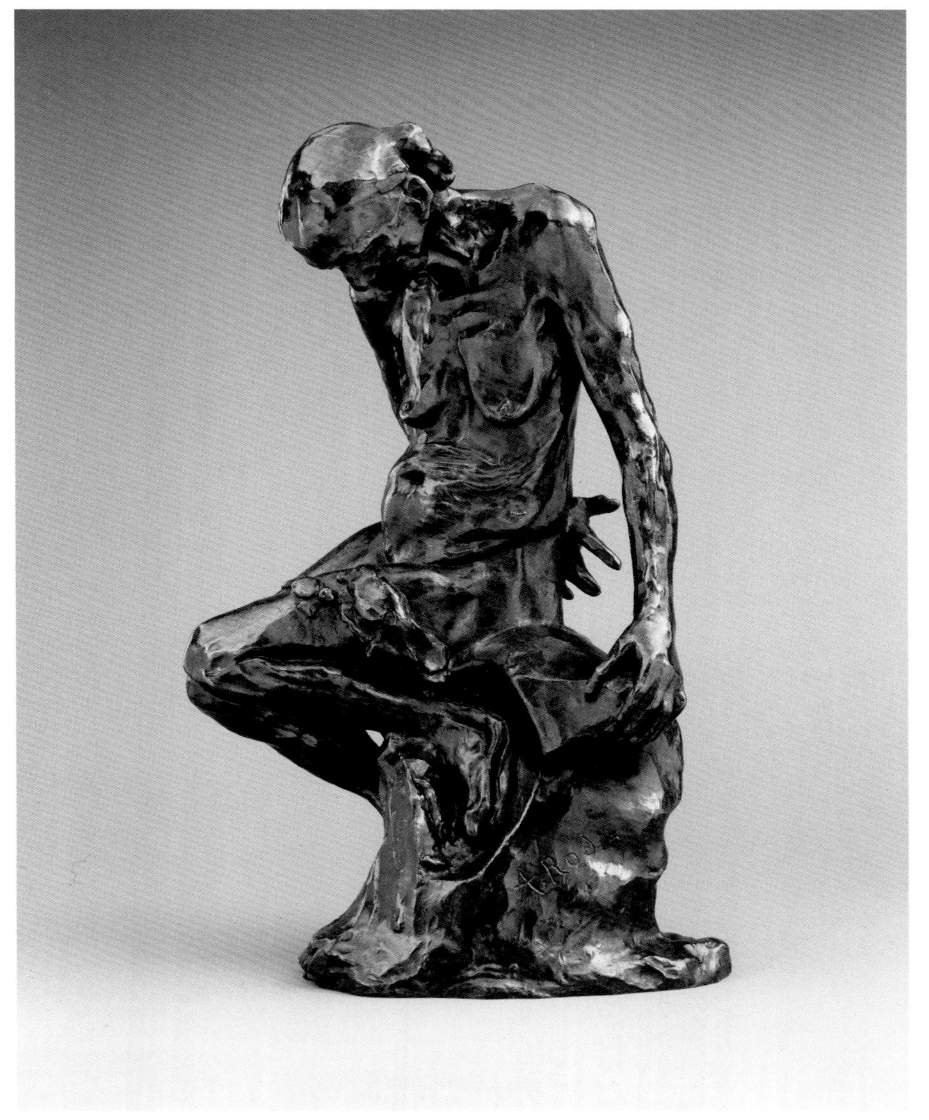

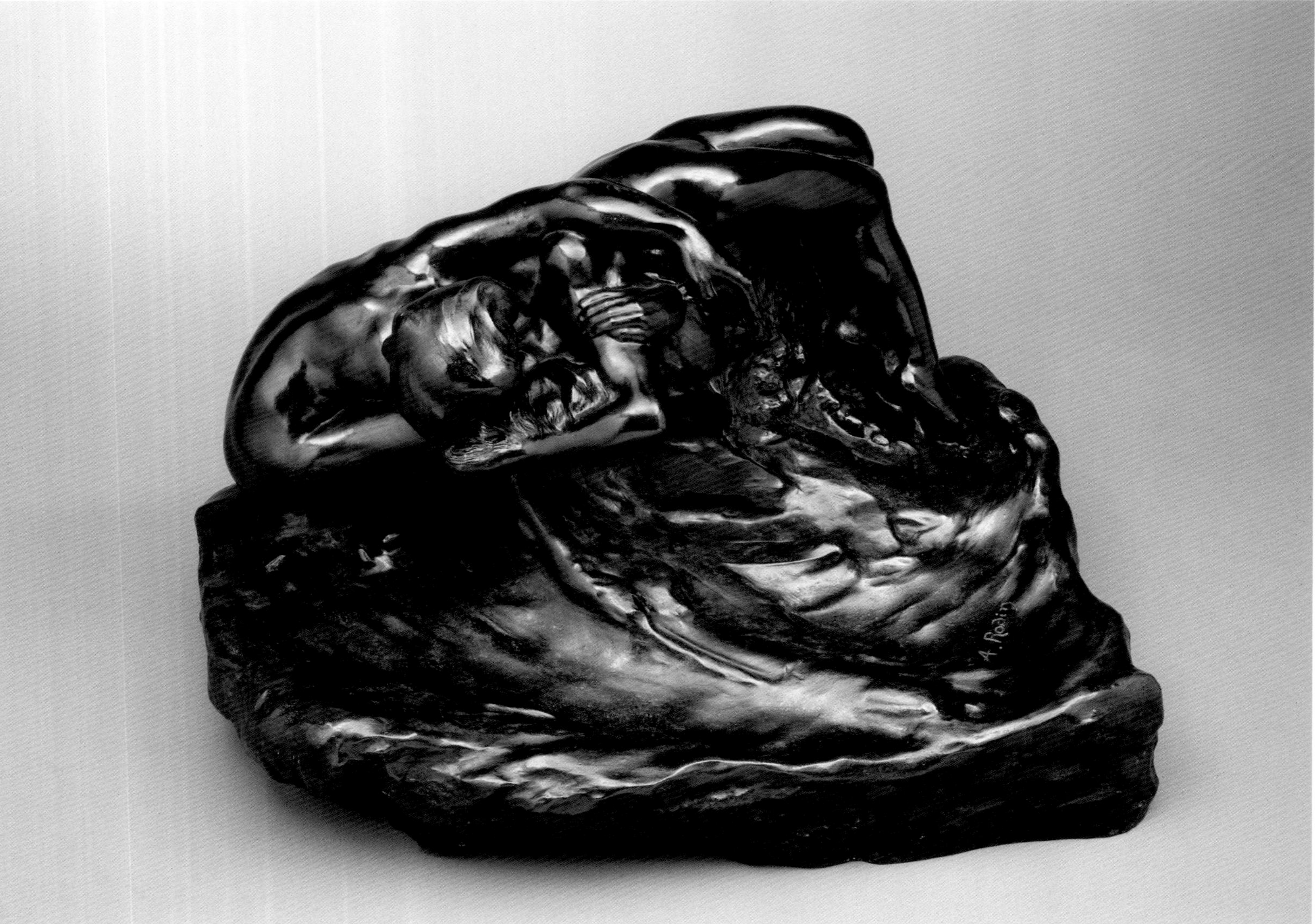

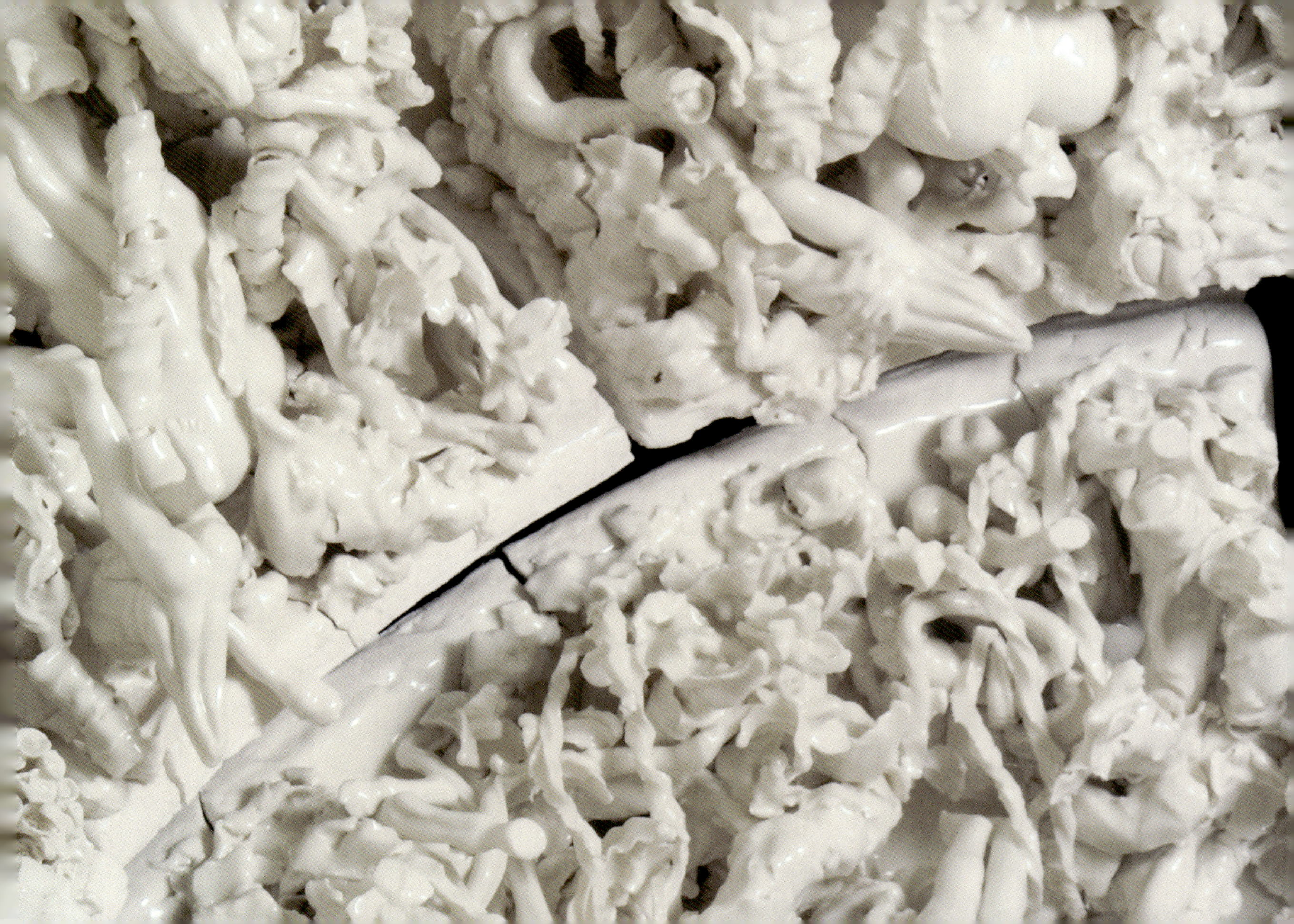

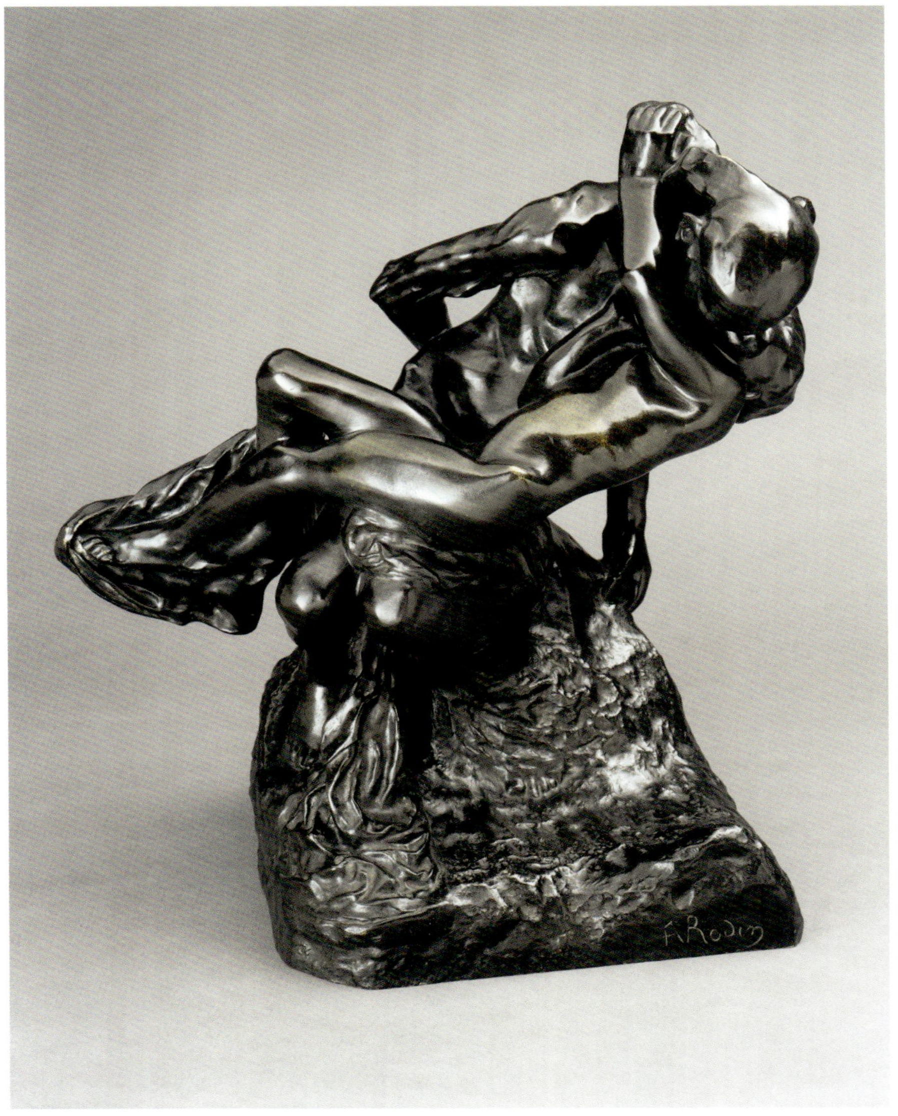

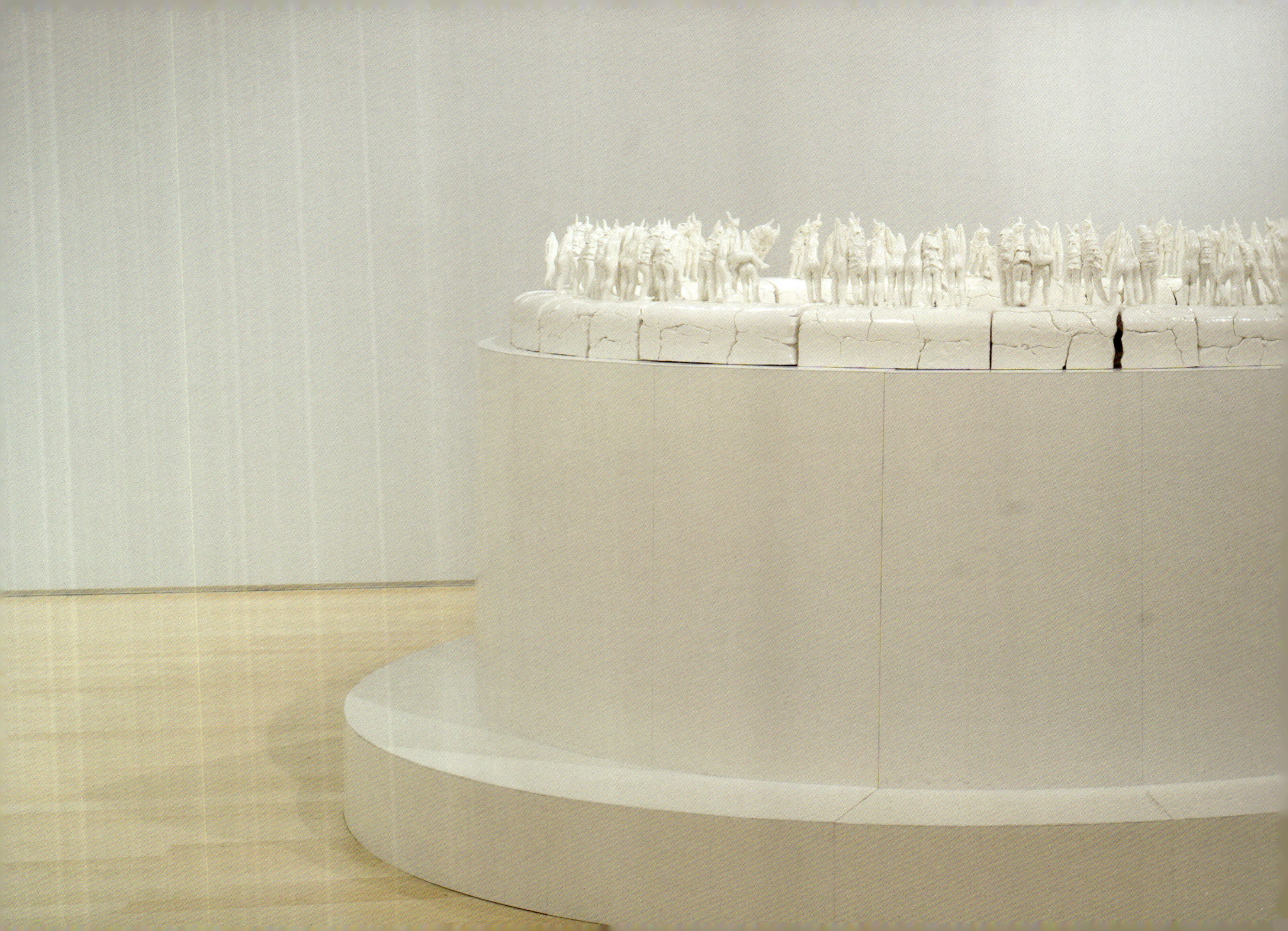

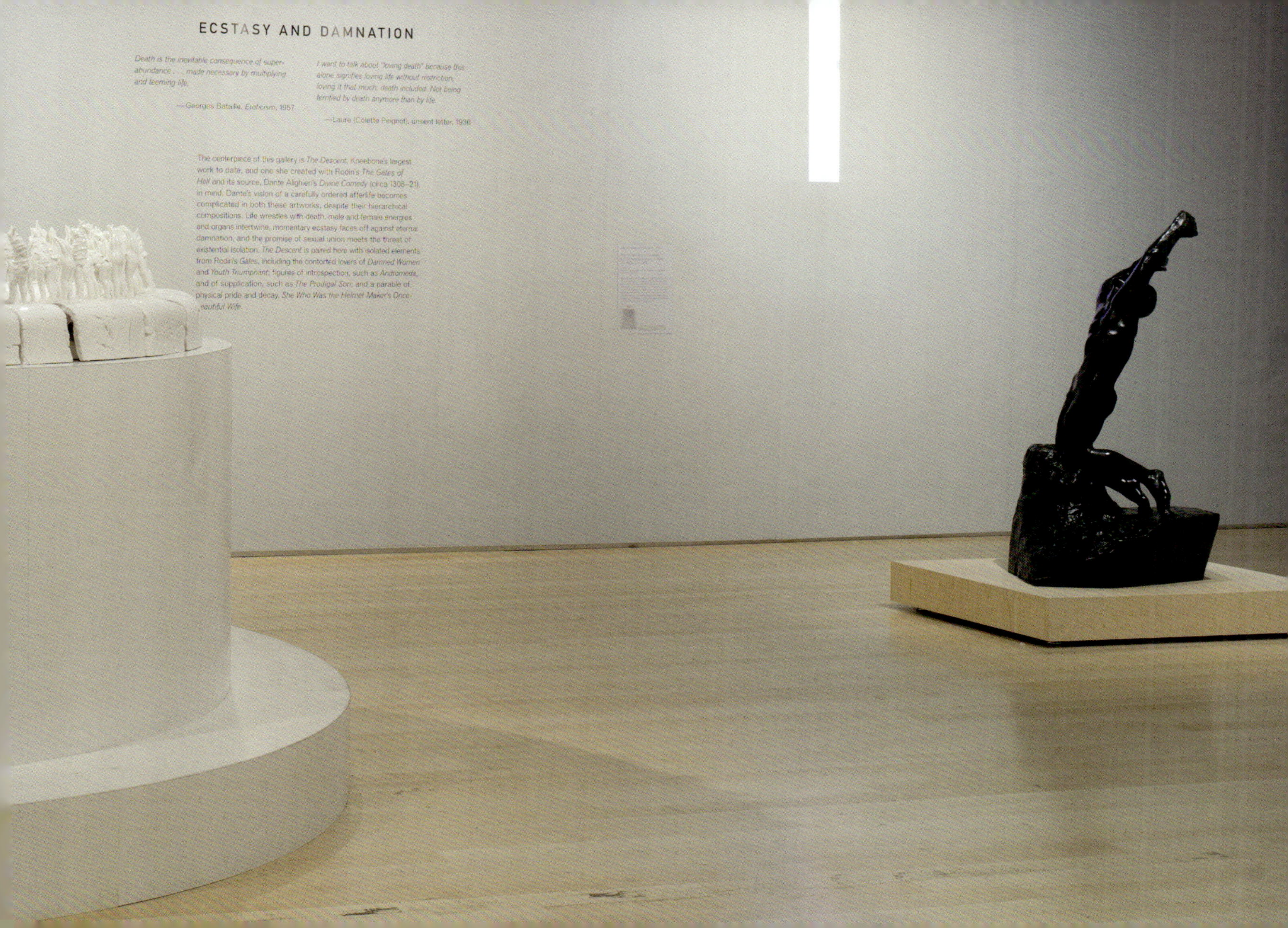

ECSTASY AND DAMNATION

Death is the inevitable consequence of super-
abundance . . . made necessary by multiplying
and teeming life.

—Georges Bataille, Eroticism, 1957

I want to talk about "loving death" because this
alone signifies loving life without restriction,
loving it that much, death included. Not being
terrified by death anymore than by life.

—Laure (Colette Peignot), unsent letter, 1936

The centerpiece of this gallery is The Descent, Kneebone's largest
work to date, and one she created with Rodin's The Gates of
Hell and its source, Dante Alighieri's Divine Comedy (circa 1308–21),
in mind. Dante's vision of a carefully ordered afterlife becomes
complicated in both these artworks, despite their hierarchical
compositions. Life wrestles with death, male and female energies
and organs intertwine, momentary ecstasy faces off against eternal
damnation, and the promise of sexual union meets the threat of
existential isolation. The Descent is paired here with isolated elements
from Rodin's Gates, including the contorted lovers of Damned Women
and Youth Triumphant; figures of introspection, such as Andromeda,
and of supplication, such as The Prodigal Son; and a parable of
physical pride and decay, She Who Was the Helmet Maker's Once-
Beautiful Wife.

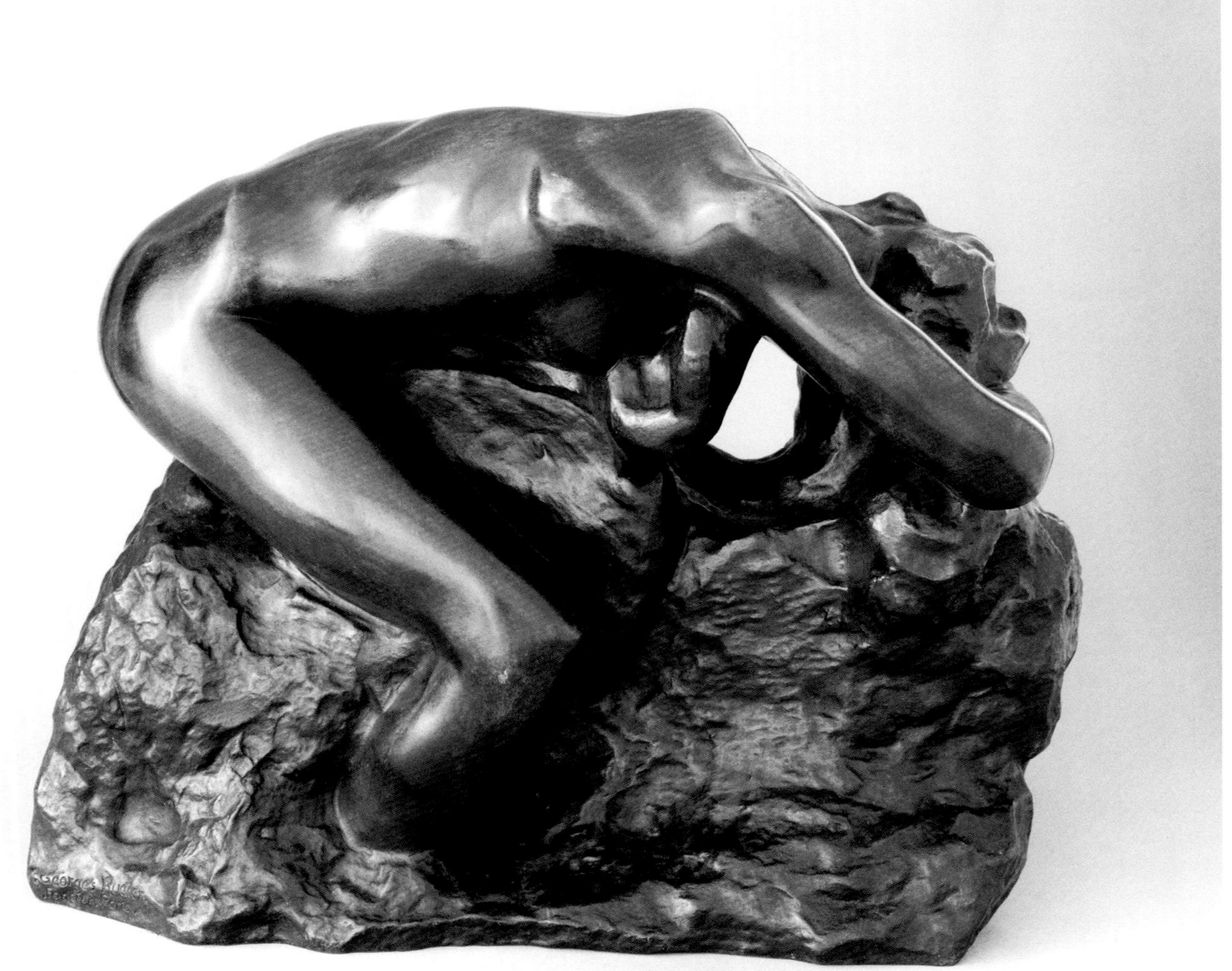

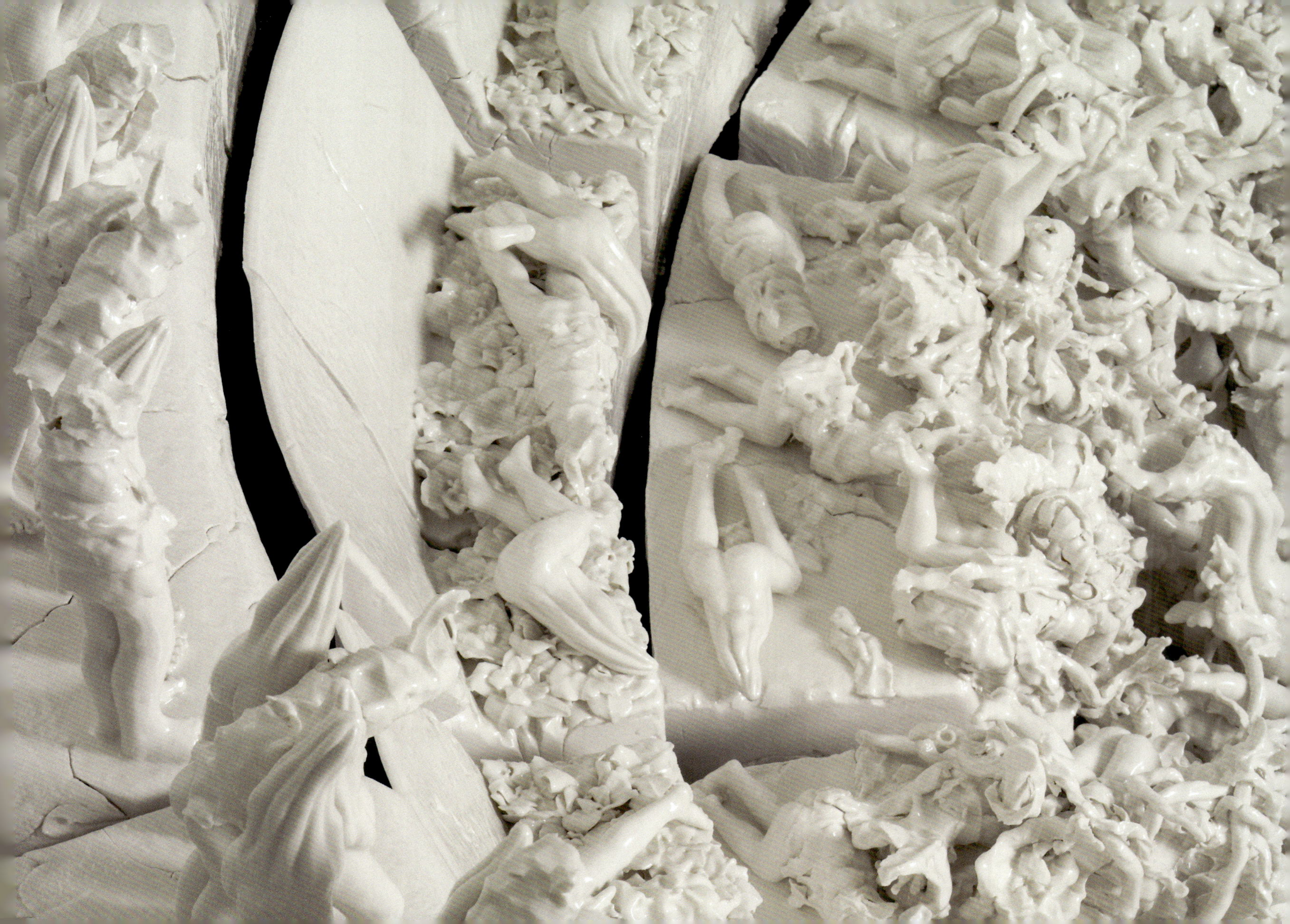

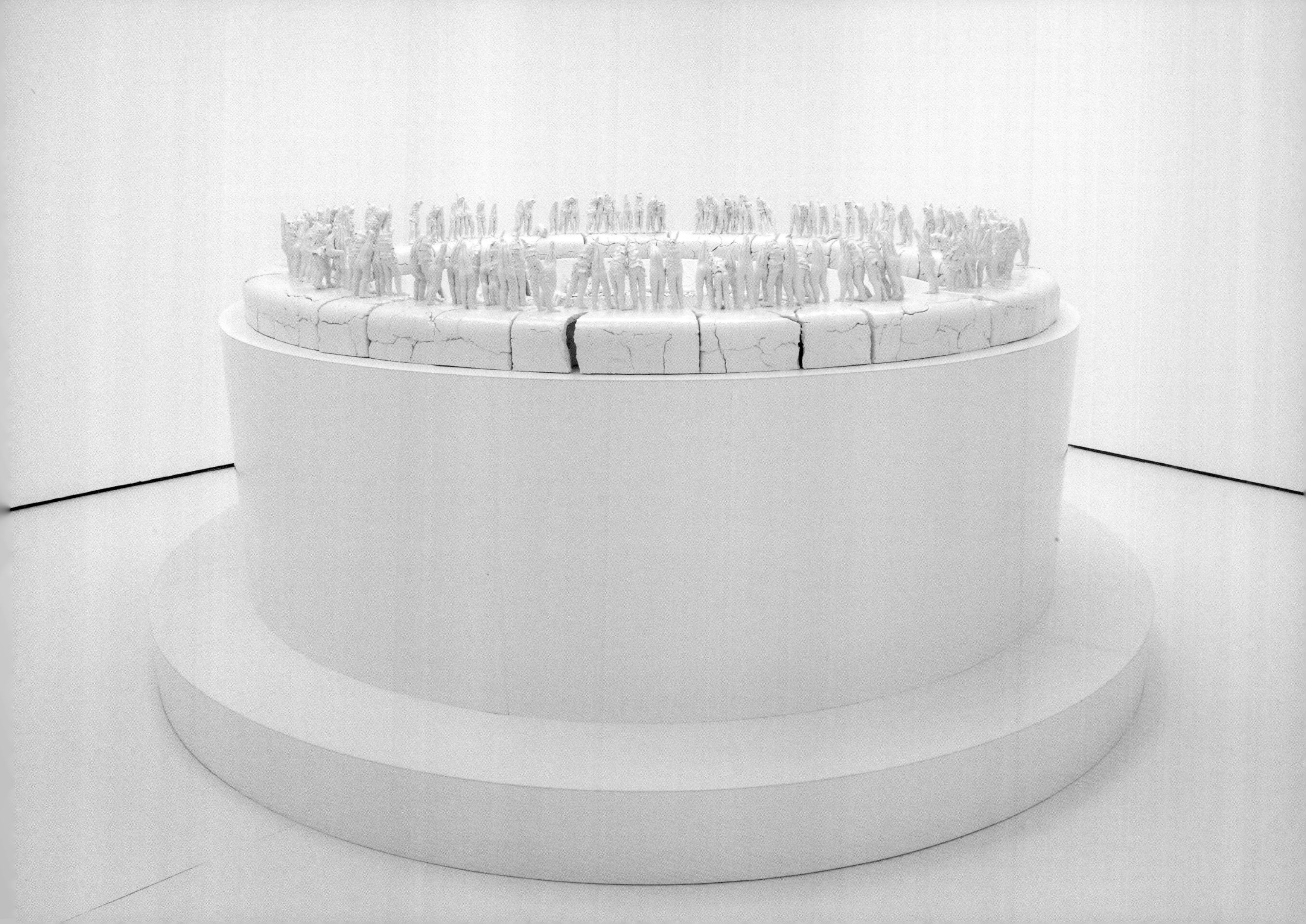

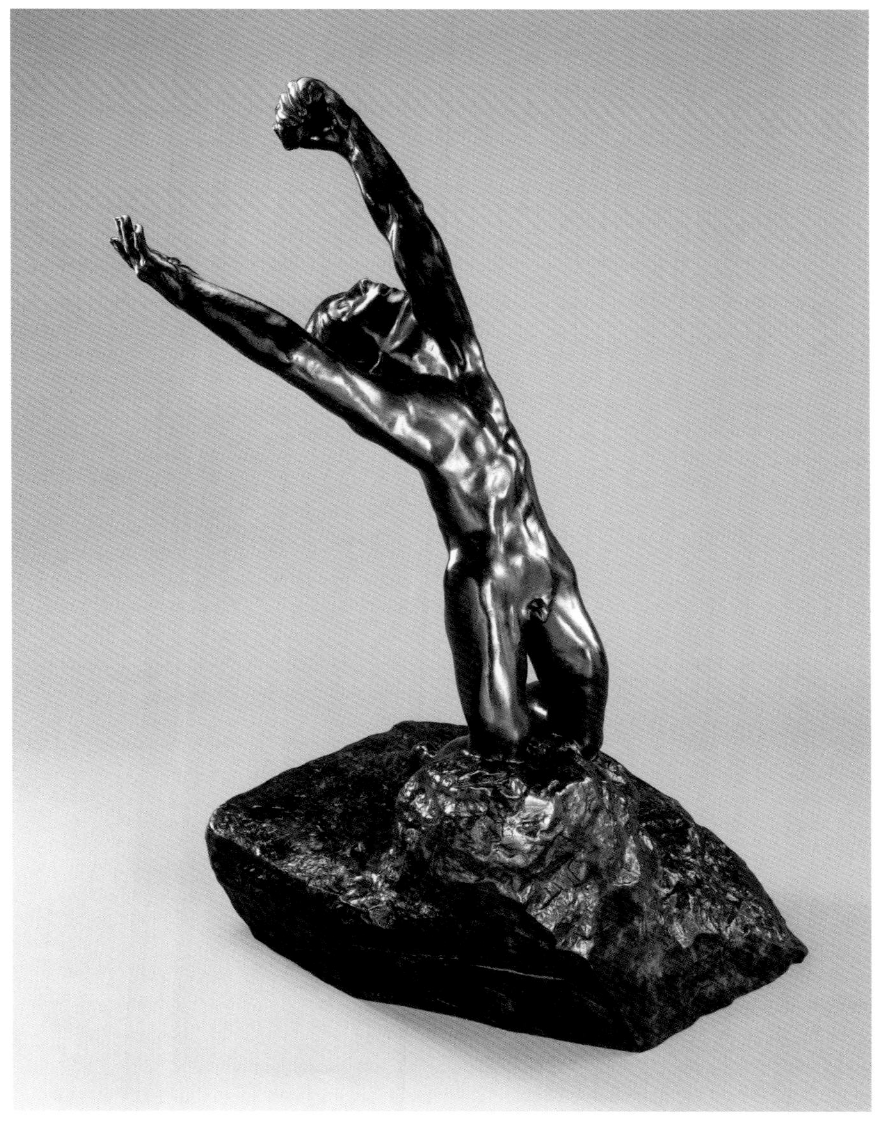

List of Works

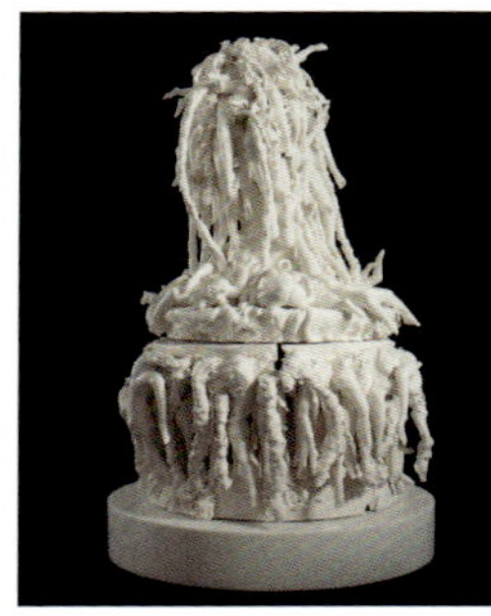

Rachel Kneebone
The Paradise of Despair
2011
Porcelain
95 × 60 × 62 cm, 37⅜ × 23⅝ × 24⁷⁄₁₆ in

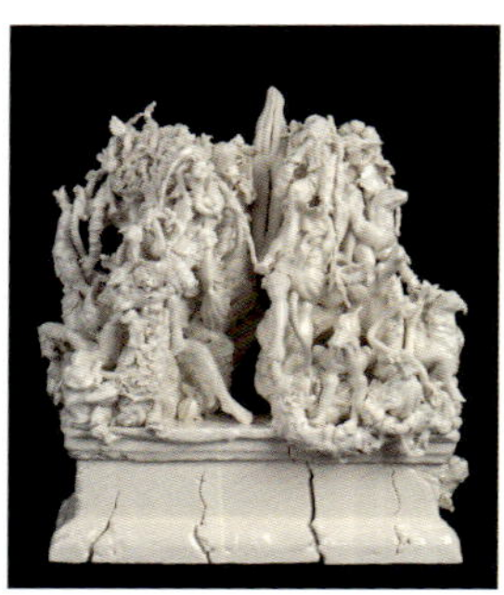

Rachel Kneebone
When I doubt I exist again
2009
Porcelain
52.7 × 30.5 × 47.6 cm, 20¾ × 12 × 18¾ in

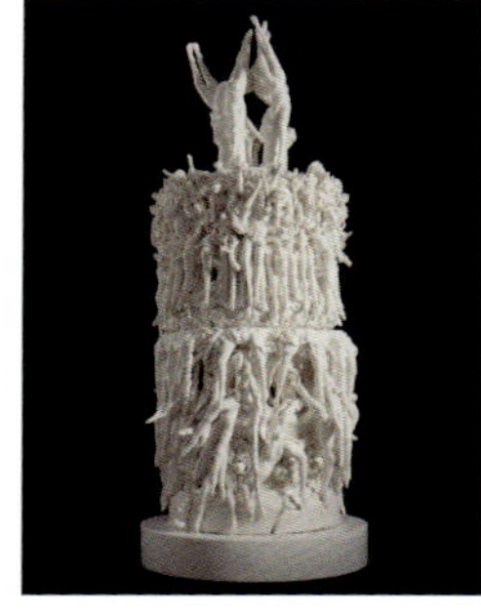

Rachel Kneebone
For Beauty's nothing but beginning of Terror
we're still just able to bear
2011
Porcelain
146 × 58 × 63 cm, 57½ × 22¹³⁄₁₆ × 24¹³⁄₁₆ in

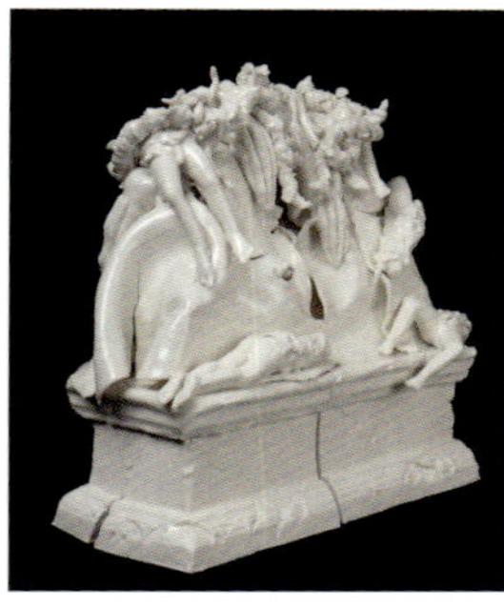

Rachel Kneebone
Blind convulsion
2009
Porcelain
43 × 26.9 × 45.2 cm, 16¹⁵⁄₁₆ × 10⁹⁄₁₆ × 17¹³⁄₁₆ in

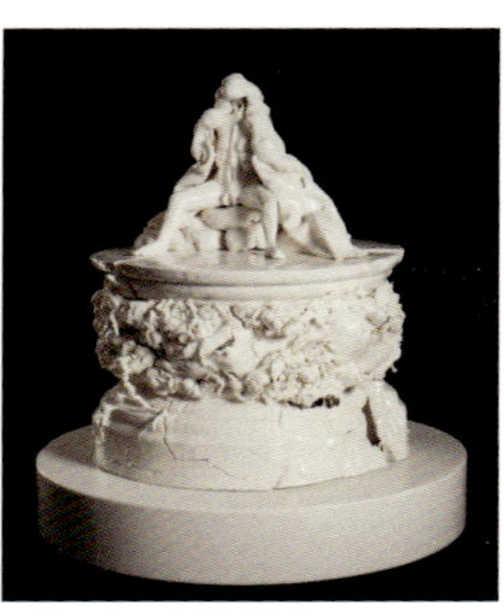

Rachel Kneebone
Eyes that look close at wounds themselves
are wounded
2010
Porcelain
54 × 47 × 47 cm, 21¼ × 18½ × 18½ in

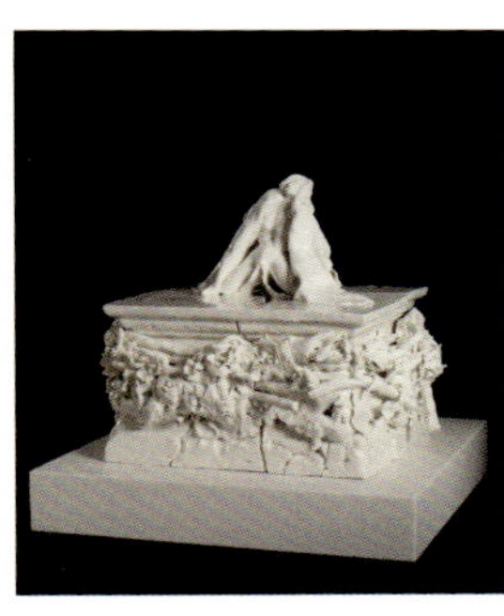

Rachel Kneebone
Mine heart is turned within me
2010
Porcelain
47 × 56 × 52 cm, 18½ × 22⁷⁄₁₆ × 20½ in

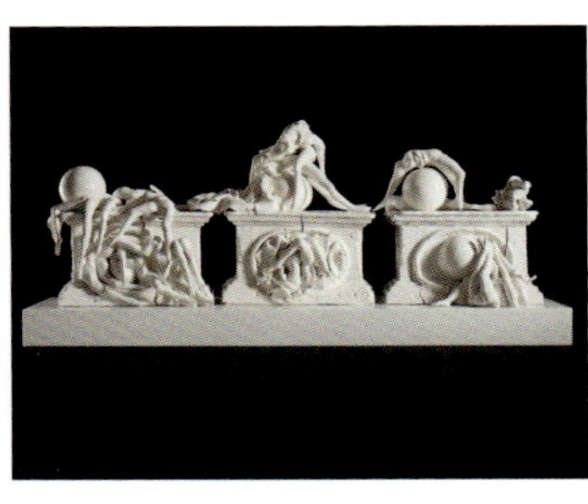

Rachel Kneebone
Still Life Triptych
2011
Porcelain
62 × 145 × 47 cm, 24⁷⁄₁₆ × 57⁷⁄₁₆ × 18½ in

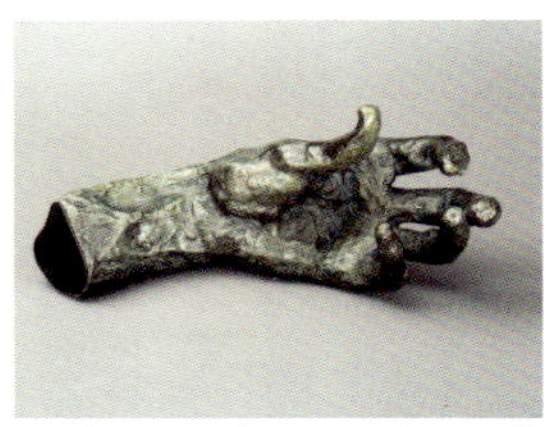

Auguste Rodin
Large Left Hand (Grande main gauche)
before 1912, date of cast unknown
Bronze
29.5 × 11.4 × 14 cm, 11⅝ × 4½ × 5½ in

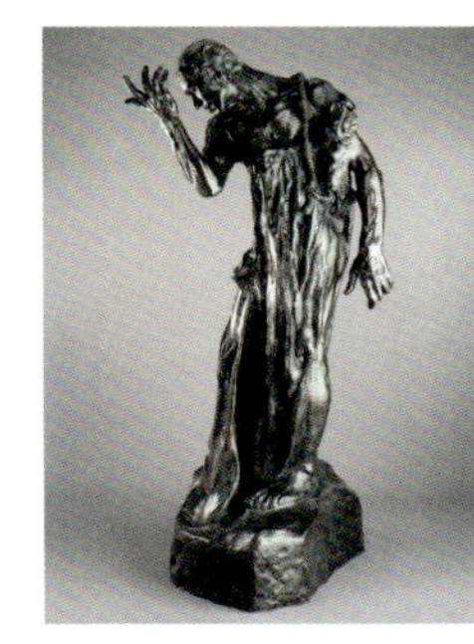

Auguste Rodin
*Pierre de Wiessant, Monumental
(Pierre de Wissant, monumental)*
1887, cast 1979
Bronze
214.9 × 116.8 × 99 cm, 84⅝ × 46 × 39 in

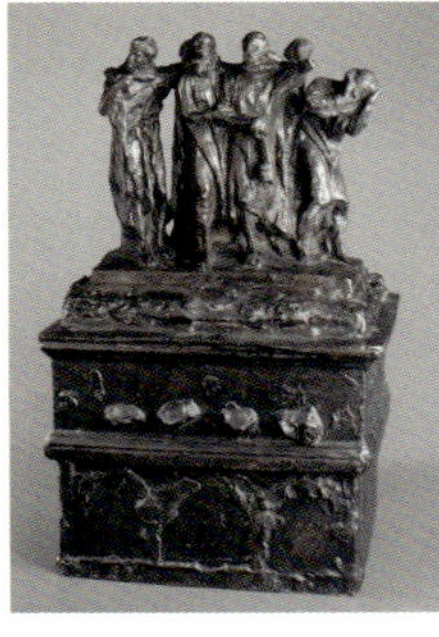

Auguste Rodin
*Monument to the Burghers of Calais, First
Maquette (Monument des Bourgeois de Calais,
première maquette)*
November 1884, cast c. 1967
Bronze
60.3 × 37.8 × 33 cm, 23¾ × 14⅞ × 13 in

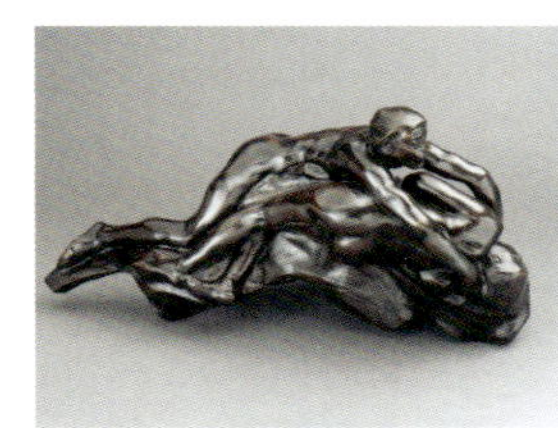

Auguste Rodin
Paolo and Francesca
Before 1886, cast 1981
Bronze
29.8 × 59 × 27 cm, 11¾ × 23¼ × 10⅝ in

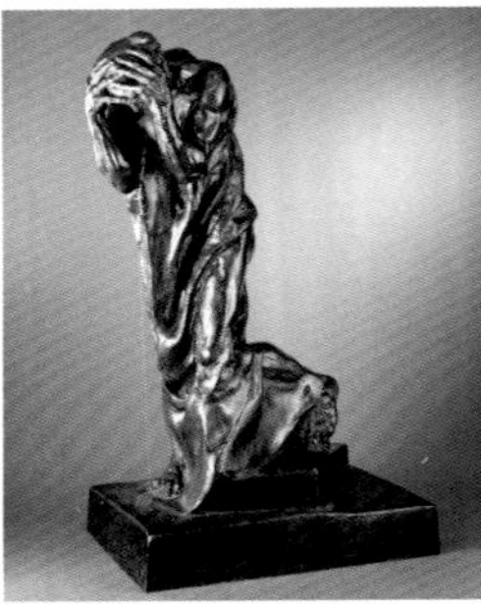

Auguste Rodin
Andrieu d'Andres, Monumental (Andrieu d'Andres, monumental)
1888, cast 1983
Bronze
199 × 127 × 85.1 cm, 78⅜ × 50 × 33½ in

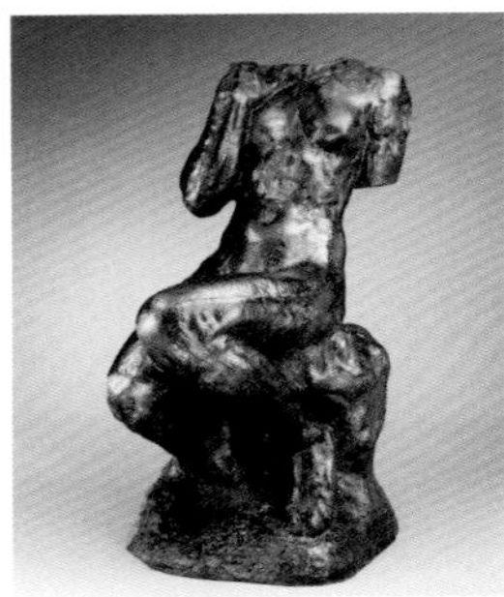

Auguste Rodin
Cybele, large model (Cybèle, grand modèle)
1905, cast 1981
Bronze
163.5 × 76.8 × 118.4 cm, 64⅜ × 30¼ × 46⅝ in

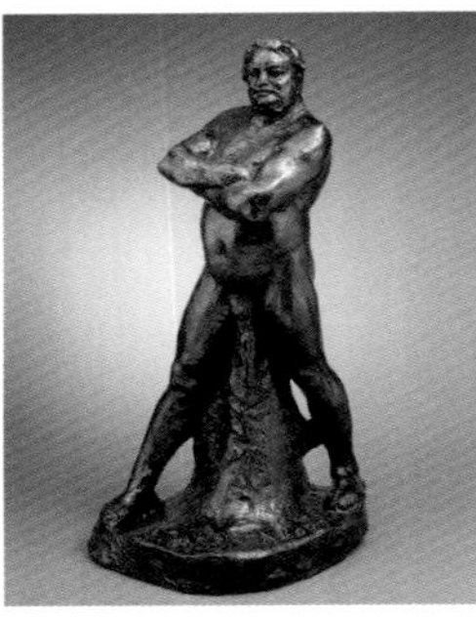

Auguste Rodin
Balzac, Nude Study C, Large Version (Balzac, étude de nu, grand modèle)
1892–1893, cast 1972
Bronze
126.7 × 48.9 × 67.3 cm, 49⅞ × 19¼ × 26½ in

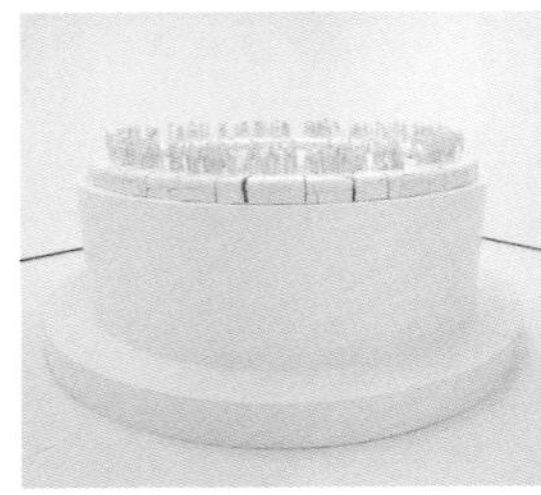

Rachel Kneebone
The Descent
2008
Porcelain
Approx. 150 × 350 cm, 59¹⁄₁₆ × 137⁵¹⁄₆₄ in

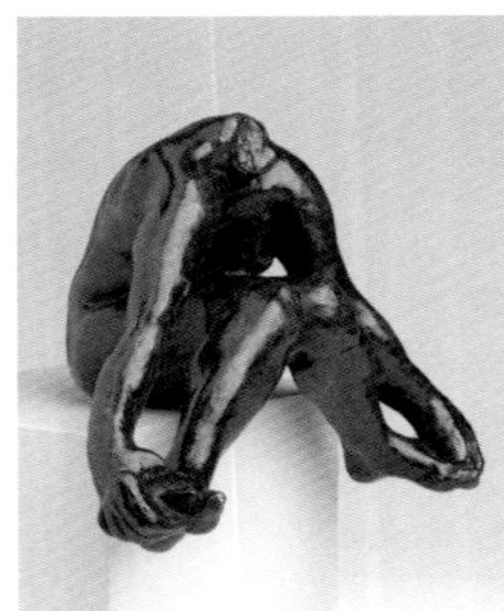

Auguste Rodin
Seated Bather with Feet Apart (Baigneuse assise, pieds écartés)
1895–1900, cast after 1972
Bronze
13 × 17.1 × 11.1 cm, 5⅛ × 6¾ × 4⅜ in

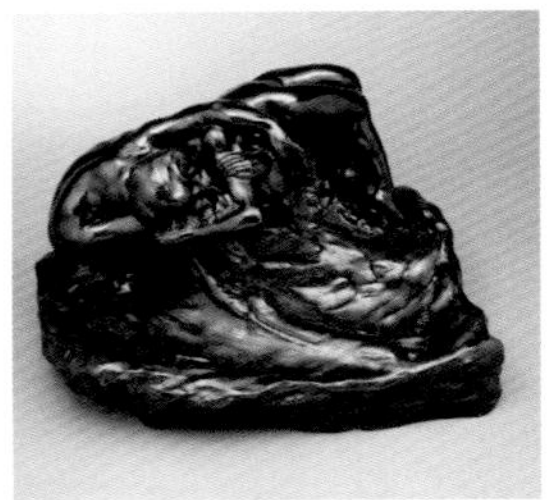

Auguste Rodin
The Fallen Angel, or Illusions Received by the Earth (La Chute d'un ange, ou Les Illusions reçues par la Terre)
By 1900, cast before 1952
Bronze
52.1 × 83.2 × 56.6 cm, 20½ × 32¾ × 22¼ in

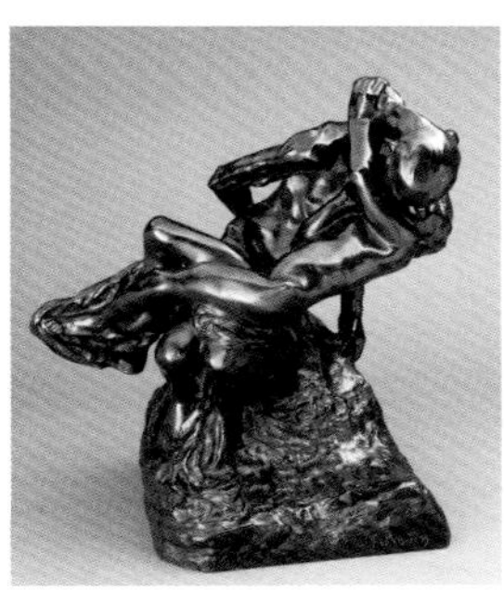

Auguste Rodin
Youth Triumphant (La Jeunesse triomphante)
1896, cast date unknown (after 1898)
Bronze
52.1 × 45.7 × 32.4 cm, 20 ½ × 18 × 12 ¾ in

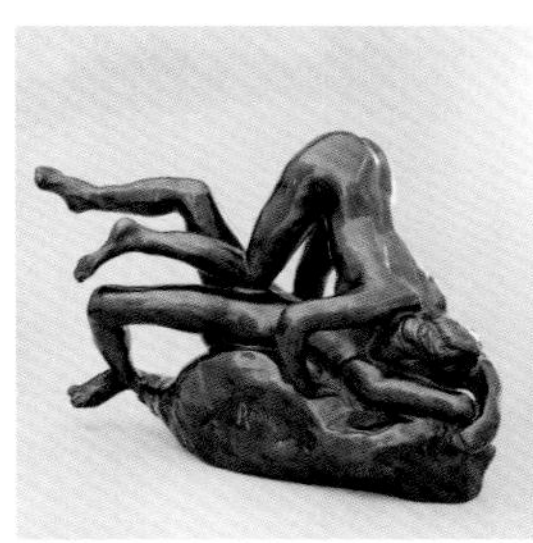

Auguste Rodin
Damned Women (Femmes damnées)
c. 1885-before 1890, cast 1979
Bronze
20 × 28.6 × 14.3 cm, 7 ⅞ × 11 ¼ × 5 ⅝ in

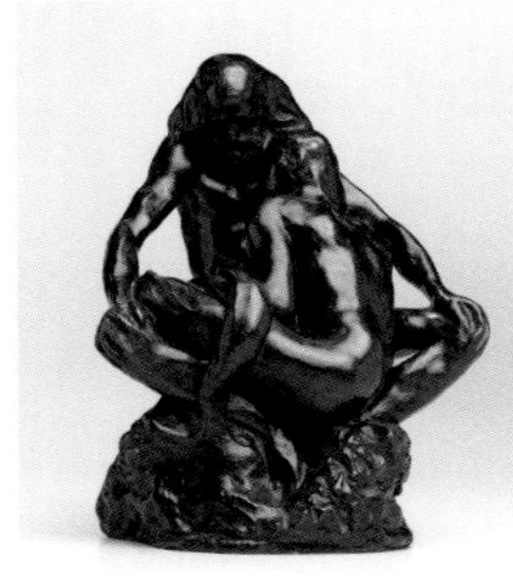

Auguste Rodin
Glaucus
1891, cast 1972
Bronze
20 × 15.5 × 12.4 cm, 7 ⅞ × 6 ⅛ × 4 ⅞ in

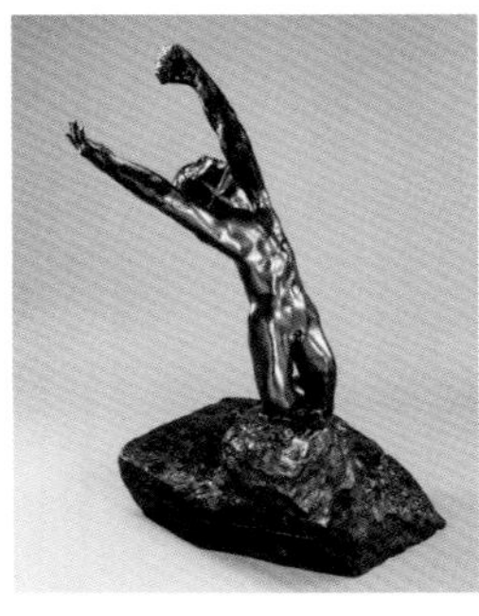

Auguste Rodin
The Prodigal Son, Large Model (L'Enfant prodigue, grand modèle)
late 1880s, cast 1969
Bronze
138.1 × 90.2 × 73 cm, 54⅜ × 35½ × 28 ¾ in

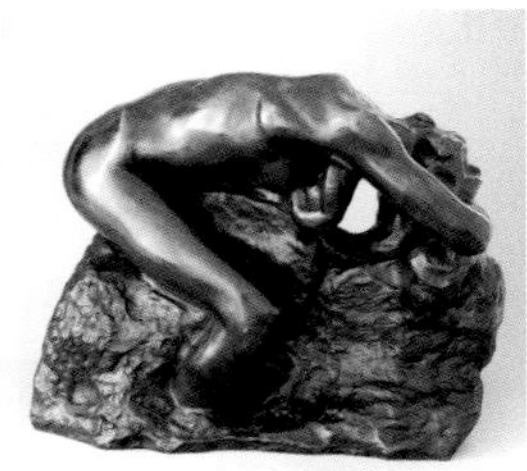

Auguste Rodin
Andromeda (Andromède)
1887, cast 1979
Bronze
26.3 × 32.1 × 19.4 cm, 10⅜ × 12⅝ × 7⅝ in

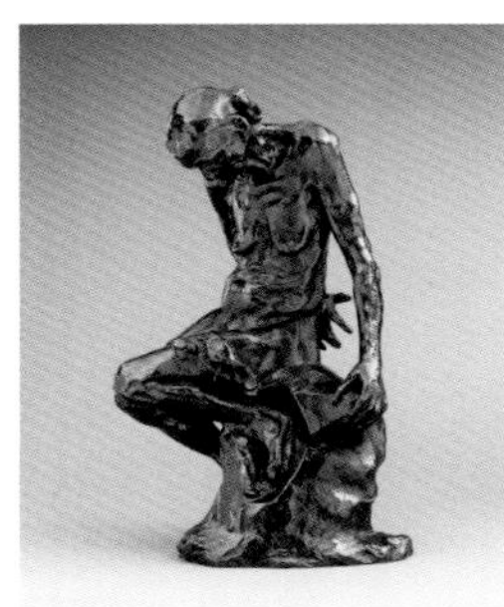

Auguste Rodin
She Who Was The Helmet Maker's Once-Beautiful Wife (Celle qui fut la belle heaulmière)
1885–1887; cast 1969
Bronze
50.2 × 33 × 24.8 cm, 19¾ × 13 × 9¾ in

Rachel Kneebone: Regarding Rodin

The Elizabeth A. Sackler Center for Feminist Art
Brooklyn Museum
January 27 – August 12, 2012

Rachel Kneebone photography by Stephen White
Auguste Rodin photography by Brooklyn Museum
Installation photography by Jon Lowe

Design by Herman Lelie and Stefania Bonelli
Works © Rachel Kneebone
Text © Ali Smith
Produced by fandg.co.uk

Published by Anomie Publishing, 2014
Anomie Publishing
London and Wakefield, UK
www.anomie-publishing.com

A catalogue record for this book is available from the British Library

ISBN: 978-1-910221-01-3
Distributed by Casemate Publishers and Book Distributors, LLC, and Casemate UK

The artist would like to thank Catherine Morris and
all her colleagues at the Brooklyn Museum, and Irene
Bradbury and everyone at White Cube for making
the show possible.

Thank you to Ali Smith for her extraordinary writing
and to Darian Leader for his invaluable support.

Many thanks also to Stephen White and Jon Lowe
for their photographs, to Herman Lelie and Stefania
Bonelli for all their work on the book's design, and to
Matthew Price for bringing it to fruition.

Anomie Publishing